BEYOND PUBLIC ARCHITECTURE

Strategies for Design Evaluations

BEYOND PUBLIC ARCHITECTURE

Strategies for Design Evaluations

Hamid Shirvani

VNR VAN NOSTRAND REINHOLD
_____ New York

Copyright © 1990 by Van Nostrand Reinhold
Library of Congress Catalog Card Number 89-48404
ISBN 0-442-31846-4

Printed in the United States of America

Van Nostrand Reinhold
115 Fifth Avenue
New York, NY 10003

Van Nostrand Reinhold International Company Limited
11 New Fetter Lane
London EC4P 4EE, England

Van Nostrand Reinhold
480 La Trobe Street
Melbourne, Victoria 3000, Australia

Nelson Canada
1120 Birchmount Road
Scarborough, Ontario M1K 5G4, Canada

16 15 14 13 12 11 10 9 8 7 6 5 4 3 2 1

Library of Congress Cataloging-in-Publication Data

Shirvani, Hamid.
    Beyond public architecture : strategies for design evaluation /
Hamid Shirvani.
        p.   cm.
    ISBN 0-442-31846-4
    1. Public architecture—Evaluation.   I. Title.
    NA9050.5.S55   1990
    352.96—dc20   89-48404
                                                    CIP

Contents

To Diane

FOREWORD
"A PROGRESS REPORT ON THE
BUILT ENVIRONMENT"

The idea of a public architecture has all but disappeared from the practice of architecture. Cities, previously seen as social settings for our human interactions, are in danger of being radically altered. This is occuring because no idea or direction is being applied to the massive construction projects now underway or to those being planned. Development has replaced planning, and the architect is in a difficult, almost paradoxical, position in relationship to such practices.

Every generation has to rethink the problems facing society. For several decades now architecture has been overly concerned with stylistic nuances and thoughts about design. Issues of zoning as it relates to the health, welfare, and well being of city dwellers have been ignored and violated consistently and vigorously. New programs requiring increased density have stretched the limit of previously conceived zoning ordinances to the point of rendering them ineffective. Overbuilding in the centers of most cities has not been carried out with consideration of the mechanical services or of light, space, and air requirements. The topography of cities changes as the layers of buildings yield to the planning and zoning requirements. These requirements are set up to take advantage of the physical attributes of a place and to insure an improved quality of life for all urban dwellers.

Hamid Shirvani's book *Beyond Public Architecture* is deeply concerned with the issues involved in decision making at the planning level. These decisions affect architecture and urban design at its most fundamental and basic levels. Philosophically Shirvani links the issues and problems of the city to the loss of craft. This is an important and an often overlooked observation, and yet it is an essential fact. Shirvani is concerned with the essence of architecture as a mystical medium which must be forced through an elaborate bureaucratic and political tangle. This must be accomplished without disturbing architecture's true essence.

Shirvani's method uses a narrative for a philosophical exploration of the problems of the past decades. The choice of 12 cities for model studies which look at economic, social, and physical characteristics is an excellent method for understanding the constructed reality as compared to the polemical thesis. It is unusual, in this period of stylistic movements, for an architect to attempt to unravel the factors that most determine the shape of our cities and buildings. This book will prove to be a valuable resource for planners, urban designers, and architects. Hamid Shirvani is giving the profession a glimpse into the future and a strong suggestion of how to regain positive control of the built environment.

GEORGE RANALLI, ARCHITECT

PREFACE

Public architecture, as it is referred to in this book, is those public spaces and places which constitute the nonprivate side of a building and its landscape and their common grounds. It is a term that has been in use for some time but has not been fully implemented. Rather, similar terms such as urban design and civic architecture are used to define the same areas of design of the built environment.

I have deliberately decided to use the term *public architecture* for several reasons, the first and most important being the position I am taking in this book: Architecture, as it is practiced in the public realm, is deficient in certain components or lacking in the processes of public planning and decision making.

The second reason is determined by my conviction that in the last three decades of practice of modern urban design, as a public planning function in particular, the field has deteriorated into a mere bureaucratic process that manufactures codified design products based on franchised models rather than generates an architecture of substance and relevance. Finally, I believe the two principal virtues of the field, social arts and craft, are being lost.

By social arts, I am referring to the social responsiveness of public architecture, the public, quasi-public, and nonprivate side of architecture—the social realm of architecture. In saying this, I am not excluding the interior, private aspects of built form, and I am not concerned simply with the public face of the architecture of the city. On the contrary, one of the issues I intend to confront in this book is depreciation of the architecture of the city into a series of catalogued design packages which impose their preconceived building exterior, overall form, and siting. What is left to the practice of architecture is basically a mechanical art, not a social art, a service to policy rather than to people.

By craft, I am speaking of the essence of architecture, that generation of spirited forceful forms, that art of exploration and experimentation with the fragments of the city which systematically has been teased out of the process of design. Many reasons can be ascribed for the loss of craft from the practice of architecture and its replacement with mechanical arts and design codification and packaging.

One reason is, of course, the ambiguity surrounding the disciplines of architecture, landscape architecture, and planning, which together contribute to the architecture of the city. Planners have become politicians or part of a political body, and architecture and landscape architecture are in a dubious and confused state. A desired balance in the dialogue of these disciplines between thinking and making, critical inquiry and the practicalities of building, craft, and market service, invention and convention has been tipped in favor of economic interests, practicality, and convention. This dialogue has been going on for decades, perhaps; however, within the last ten years it has begun to echo the discontent of professionals with this imbalance. With a broadening and proliferation of the intellectual and critical base, the dialogue has moved toward an application of theory in the built realm, with architecture itself carrying on a dialogue between convention and invention.

The evolution of such dialogue may seem more reasonable if I put it into perspective. Since the Industrial Revolution, there has been a frenzy for new inventions and creations, both good and bad, aimed at the public realm of architecture and the city. However, with the incremental notions of the 1960s that have strongly dominated the field, much of the push toward experimentation and innovation has been replaced with nostalgia and convention. This has become an overwhelming force in shaping the American city. This phenomenon is certainly the product of postmodernism. Similarly, the discipline of city planning has experienced a series of revolutionary changes which came to a halt in the 1960s when it fell into the same postmodernistic slump; conventional models have squelched invention and exploration in the field. Economic support for public planning and discontinuation of federal programs and funds have tended to perpetuate those conventions based on market-oriented service models rather than on innovative approaches aimed at public and social needs.

Proceeding from the above premises, this book attempts to demonstrate the current state of the "art" of public architecture by a close examination of the public institution, its processes and mechanisms, its form and contents, and its goals and directions in regard to the architecture of the city. In so doing, I question the existing models and identify their inadequacies in achieving an architecture of the city within the public realm. My conclusion is that the postmodern approach to urban design and its attempts at re-creating the city of the past in the last three decades has been detrimental to the architecture of the city and to the public institution as a whole. In conjunction to this analysis and critique, I also will offer some suggestions for areas of change. In taking such a position, I am acknowledging a criticism of my earlier work on the subject as contributing to the postmodern phenomenon (Shirvani, 1985: *Urban Design Process*, Van Nostrand Reinhold).

For this purpose, I have selected 12 cities and a town across the United States with different geographic, economic, and social characteristics: Baltimore, Maryland; Dallas, Texas; Indianapolis, Indiana; Irvine, California; Kansas City, Missouri; Lincoln, Nebraska; Minneapolis, Minnesota; Portland, Oregon; San Diego, California; San Francisco, California; Seattle, Washington; and Vail, Colorado. These cities have been identified as differing examples of the postmodern applications of urban design as public policy *or* design of the public realm.

The Introduction is a brief history of the postmodern period, outlining the main events leading to the formation of a variety of models and techniques. I will discuss the fundamental premises of these models, their faulty underlying assumptions, and their multiple, and at the same time, conflicting goals. I will establish a framework of analysis based on form and content of the existing models in practice.

Hamid Shirvani

ACKNOWLEDGMENTS

The origins of this book lie in my long-standing interest in architecture of the city, and the research began some years ago. The actual writing did not begin until 1986, when I was appointed dean of the School of Architecture and Planning at the University of Colorado at Denver. When I assumed the position at UC-Denver, I was under the impression that I could maintain my research and writing at the level as before. I soon discovered that my impression was grossly inaccurate. The book took at least one extra year to complete.

Many individuals have contributed to the content of this book in various ways. These included colleagues, friends, and students in the School of Architecture and Planning at UC-Denver and elsewhere. First of all, I am grateful to the many graduate students who took my urban design course in spring 1987. The materials and other information these students collected about the twelve cities and the many stimulating discussions we had were extremely beneficial to me. My colleagues, Ned Collier, Paul Saporito, and Frederick Steiner, read various chapters of this book. I am indebted to them for their helpful advice and comments. I am particularly grateful to my research assistant, Karla Mueller, and my editor, Nancy L. Daniels, for their invaluable contribution and their assistance in preparation of the manuscript. Finally, for meticulous typing, I greatly appreciate the work of Judy Strecker, who handled the difficult task of preparing the various drafts of the manuscript.

Introduction:
Architecture, City, and
the Institution

Ever since the Industrial Revolution and its effects on the structure and character of the city, the nature of architecture in the public realm has always played a crucial role in the history of both architecture and planning. The welfare of society and of the public at large have been the concern of both European functionalists and utopian visionaries in dealing with city planning and architecture. American public institutions followed suit, from the laissez-faire based City Beautiful Movement, which relied on European models and attempted to beautify the existing city fabric, to the birth of city planning by government in the early 1900s. Attempts to deal with the changes brought about by the industrialization of the city became essential goals for many public figures, architects, and town planners. These changes included the "pluralistic definition of citizenship, continuing immigration and associated assimilation, social repolarization, . . . separation of home and work, and a profound reorganization of urban economic activity."[1]

Early in this century, the public involvement in the urban environment became a governmental issue. Several ambitious steps were taken toward the deprivatization of public space, ranging from the creation of civic monuments, public parks and park systems, public libraries, and civic centers to planning efforts. This led to master plans and comprehensive plans and in turn to the development of mechanisms of implementation such as zoning and other types of land-use controls. Some of the efforts have yielded successful products and positive impacts, while others have remained uninspired and have effected negative results.

Regardless of these attempts at "popular planning," the private sector has continuously determined the American city building enterprise. An exception came in the late 1950s and early 1960s with the advent of urban renewal. Its attempts to generate revenue through the wholesale destruction of low-income communities created such a stir within the public sector that it opened the first opportunities for planners and urban designers to directly intervene in the process of urban development and city rebuilding. Out of urban renewal and public intervention came the whole notion of urban design as the guardian of public character and civic pride. However, as urban design practice has evolved in the period of postmodernism, it has become more the guardian of visual coherence and quality of the urban fabric than the champion of the public good.[2] Like the City Beautiful Movement, it relies on the beautification of an urban layout which is determined to a great extent by the economic framework.[3] This economic determination is a critical issue as it is often at odds with the best interests of the public.

The "architect-as-cosmetician" is a very different scenario from that of the 1950s. Architects traditionally had an extensive role in city planning and in the determining of the city's physical form; great cities and urban environments were the result of architects' conceptions rather than developers' interests. As cities became ever more complex, the architect's place within the overall design and ordering of the physical environment diminished and became more specialized. Over the last 30 years, architects have been concerning themselves with the design of fragmented pieces of the urban fabric, beautification, corporate symbolism, and real estate development. Today we find that those nonphysical planners who have been critical of the elitism associated with the architecture of the sixties have become more allied with developers than architects have ever been.[4]

This notion of urban design, as we have come to think of it, began with two general approaches: project and process. The project approach first began with urban renewal projects in the 1960s and grew into the development of large-scale real estate projects. The impetus for such an approach was twofold. Certain large-scale development projects can act like incubators for new business, thus satisfying economic concerns while bringing life to the city in hopes of rebuilding the city of old. The fundamental task, then, is the development of projects such as the rehabilitation of aging urban districts for retail or mixed use, the development of a convention center or hotel complex, pedestrian amenities, or urban residential development. Usually the products are conceptual plans, with the "large-scale architectural plan" then translated into the written and graphic guidelines that constitute the structure of real estate development and the enhancement of the architectural quality of the city.[5]

The process-oriented approach began with the manipulation of city zoning ordinances and the establishment of economic incentives in return for certain public-oriented amenities such as plazas and arcades in an attempt to satisfy both economic interest and public policy. This approach grew into a fever for design guidelines, advisory and legislative, or for city zoning and other land-use regulation. Indeed, over the last 30 years the practice of urban design has become less interested in the physical structure of cities and more occupied with those elements of process; "urban design has become a means towards an end rather than a goal or undertaking in itself."[6]

Both approaches have a common goal, to bring back the old city—to rebuild the city within the contextual framework of the old city grid and historic buildings. Unfortunately, the guidelines that inevitably emerge from these models may succeed in creating "nothing more than imagistic clonings of arcadian illusionism, following architecture of blind precedent and seeking compatibility with immediate context instead of engaging in analysis beyond the immediately defined boundaries of the site."[7] However, the goals of historic continuity have been tainted by another often conflicting goal, the generation of tax dollars for the city. Development means people, and people mean dollars. This inherent dichotomy between the two alternate agendas of physical enhancement and economic interests has made for questionable achievements at best. An example of the result of this jumble of programs is the "historic" shopping district which, while retaining the "age" of the buildings involved, is simply a collection of franchised businesses.

Therefore, both approaches attempt to take a middle road by dividing the city into zones of both historic and use-specific districts, applying the most orthodox guidelines to the historic district and dollar-generative guidelines to other zones. Can economic development be equated with meaningful design? And, in making this equation, are we running the risk of letting the character of our cities be determined by market-oriented models resulting in franchised design packages? The so-called mixed-use and waterfront developments, malls, arcades, etc., are the products of this postmodern phenomenon of city revival.

In order to investigate the nature and content of this postmodern approach to urban design, I have developed a critical framework based on elements presently found in practice. As I have mentioned, the use of the term *public architecture* rather than *urban design* is a question of scope: the broad range of activities and functions that are grouped under the umbrella of urban design versus architecture of the city, the focus of this book. Public architecture refers to the public realm of architecture and is considered a part of urban design practice today, but it is not the main focus of urban design. In fact, one of my central criticisms in this book is that the postmodern approach of urban design has failed to deal with the fact that it has taken a back seat or operates primarily in service to economic development. My position is that architecture and city planning have become intertwined into the conventional approach of real estate development; as a result there is a divergence between architecture and the city.[8]

Having stated this, let me outline the critical framework, inductive in nature and based on existing models now being utilized in the 12 cities. The key to this investigation is "public": how the public is informed about architecture, how the public realm is defined, what processes are used to evaluate the resultant product, and whether the products resulting from this process of public interaction constitute an architecture of the city. This is the range of questions with which we are concerned. Our intention is to examine the processes of public guidelines, evaluation, and promotion of architecture *of* and *in* the city. This model encompasses five components:

Public evaluation
Bureaucratic processes
Framework and actors
Context
Substantive elements

This grouping of components is primarily a reflection of existing models in practice and is not necessarily my preference for critical analysis of the city.

Chapters 1 through 5 will each cover one of the components above, and each focuses on the study of the 12 cities from that perspective. In considering public evaluation (Chapter 1), we examine the range and scope of design evaluation processes based on three common categories: architectural concept, environmental impact, and planning and building regulation. A comparative analysis not only of the depth of these processes in the 12 cities but also of their fundamental underpinnings is presented. The discussion of bureaucratic processes (Chapter 2) outlines four basic models for the administrative organization handling public evaluation processes and reflects the degree of variance in our 12 cities. This line of examination is continued in the study of the actors involved in the evaluation process and the framework within which they operate (Chapter 3). Who makes up the evaluation body, and how do they fit into the overall organizational structure of the city?

Chapters 4 and 5 take a closer look at the context of the guidelines themselves and the substance of the elements which is judged under these guidelines. How is the architecture of the city achieved, and what is the result of this method of achievement? Chapter 6 is an attempt to reconstruct the particular diagnoses identified in all the chapters and to develop an overall critical outlook on the status of the architecture of the city based on the postmodern approach. Chapter 7 offers an alternative proposal for public architecture and the architecture of the city.

REFERENCE NOTES

1. Mark La Gory and John Pipkin, *Urban Social Space* (Belmont, CA: Wadsworth Publishing, 1981), 272.
2. Edward Relph, *The Modern Urban Landscape* (Baltimore: Johns Hopkins University Press, 1987), 229.

3. Mario Manieri-Elia, "Toward an 'Imperial City'," in *The American City, from the Civil War to the New Deal,* trans. Barbara Luigia La Penta (Cambridge, MA: MIT Press, 1979), 106-107.

4. Hamid Shirvani, "Architecture and the City: The Divergence," in *Who Designs America?* A selection of papers presented at the 76th Annual Meeting of the Association of Collegiate Schools of Architecture, 1988, ed. Ronald Filson and Tim McGinty (Washington, D.C.: Association of Collegiate Schools of Architecture, 1988), 136-137.

5. Ibid., 136.

6. Ibid., 135.

7. Hamid Shirvani, "City as Artifact," *Urban Design International* 8 (1988):3.

8. Hamid Shirvani, "Architecture Versus Franchised Design," *Urban Design and Preservation Quarterly* 11, No. 2/3 (1988):2-8; idem, "Architecture and the City: The Divergence," 135-141.

Chapter 1

PUBLIC EVALUATION

In this chapter, we will analyze design evaluation in terms of three categories of process in order to extract a particular city's public architecture from the whole of city policy. We will look for the evaluation categories of architectural concept, environmental impact, and planning and building regulation. Such a categorization is essential to establish exactly what a city means when it refers to having a design evaluation process. We must determine if that design evaluation is complete; that is, does it cover and embrace all three areas; or does it actually focus on only one or more specific categories?

My argument in this chapter is that although a comprehensive process covers all three categories, the notions upon which these often complicated procedures are based will determine their success. Therefore, in addition to completeness of the categories covered, the fundamental analytical basis of these categories are in question regardless of how holistic the process is.

To begin, let us outline the components of a total design evaluation process encompassing the three categories. Then we will examine the 12 case studies to determine the completeness of design evaluation at work in these cities and whether this completeness has a real foundation reflected in the architecture of the city. To many architects and designers it may seem unnecessary to describe these categories as fully as we intend to do. The very fact that these categories have become so familiar and entrenched in the architecture and planning vocabulary is reason enough for us to take another look. We must delineate each category in order to establish a framework for comparison.

In order to initiate a development project, the first stage is presentation of the architectural design concept based on a specific program, site, context and characteristics, financial resources, functional requirements, etc. The architect's role is often restricted to the development of an architectural design concept which fits into the program needs and the site context, while meeting the city's basic requirements for a project. The city, it is hoped, has made it possible for architects to receive guidance on the urban design requirements and frameworks prior to development programming.

The concern at this time is the overall architectural design concept. Discussion may include, but is not limited to, urban design elements such as land use, building form, circulation and parking, landscape, pedestrian ways, and other elements that the city has identified. In addition, specific functional requirements are important: Are sidewalks required? Are neon lights allowed? Must a structure at this location have retail space at ground level and residential space provided along with the other usages planned? Does the building have to conform to preservation standards? Architects who have researched the city's procedures already are informed about these details. They may even be aware of the possibility of reviewer biases so that some criticisms may be forestalled.

Environmental impact studies certainly are an integral part of design evaluation in the early stages; accordingly, this activity forms our second category of design evaluation. We may have to look more carefully to find evidence that this process is going on in our 12 cities. Sometimes the evaluators handle environmental concerns informally, relying on previous experience rather than written specifications. Let us not dismiss such methods offhand but instead look for consistent results.

The range of questions raised in this regard are: Will runoff from the area adversely affect surrounding buildings and open spaces? Is the building situated on the lot so as to prevent shaded plazas while the building is in use, or will it adversely shade pedestrian ways or other buildings? Will occupancy of the building put a burden on education, water, sewerage, and transportation facilities? Will the new project cause additional traffic in the neighborhood, taxing street capacity and making it dangerous for children? An environmental impact assessment may need to be made and reported so as to identify specifically the impacts of a project on its surroundings.

The third category of design evaluation, traditionally evaluated by a large number of cities and currently used to determine the success of a proposed project, is in the area of planning and building regulation. With this step in place in addition to or above and beyond the evaluation of the architectural concept and environmental impact, the proposed project has to meet the requirements of city zoning ordinances and other building code requirements. The city will be looking to see whether the floor area ratio (FAR) requirement, height restrictions, setback and frontage requirements, and other standards have been met. Determining that the proposed development meets structural requirements and that the materials selected are appropriate and in accordance with the fire code requirements, etc., are also important aspects of the design evaluation process. If the checking of building details and the issuing of permits are more than a rubber stamp procedure, this stage can become a vital part of design evaluation dealing with issues of public safety.

Our case studies will show how the cities are approaching design evaluation and whether there are cities which include all three categories in their evaluation process. What categories are used most by the cities, and how do they approach each of them? Irvine, San Francisco, and San Diego appear to have the three-part design evaluation we have determined above, partly due to California environmental law. All 12 cities have an architectural concept evaluation and planning and building regulations. It is in the middle step of the design evaluation, environmental impact assessment, that we find the most differences among the cities. Absence of a separate and organized environmental impact assessment or an ad hoc approach is most puzzling and will require some explanation and discussion.

1.1 ARCHITECTURAL CONCEPT REVIEW

As the most important aspect of public architecture, it is interesting to examine the 12 case studies to determine what the interpretations of this category are in practice. How are they different; or perhaps, more appropriately, how are they similar and in some instances even modeled after each other? Examination clearly reveals that this category is basically a three-dimensional manifestation of the cities' zoning ordinances. Thus, as with ordinances, the underlying premises are also very much the same. Let's page through our cases.

Irvine

In Irvine, California, the majority of the land is or has been owned by The Irvine Company which has its own Urban Design Division. As a result, the company's development reveals a strong concern for urban design principles. In addition, the numerous homeowners' associations in the city have architectural and design review boards which deal with design-oriented issues. The city's Community Development Department makes available information concerning their Conditional Use Permits, Zoning Compliance Review, and the Code Compliance Process.

In the comprehensive study of Wallace, McHarg, Roberts, and Todd, "Urban Design Implementation Plan: City of Irvine Horizon Year Policies" (1977), jointly financed by the city and The Irvine Company, it is evident that the city of Irvine has a strong commitment to urban design (Figures 1.1 and 1.2). Yet it has been developed by mirroring the concerns of The Irvine Company. The result of such an alliance between city and developer is the creation of cities which are "not so much designed any more as managed."[1]

The Irvine Company has detailed plans for each area it has developed. Consider one of the latest, Westpark. For example, in the "Design Guidelines:

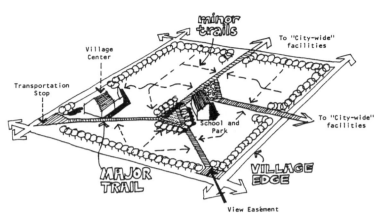

Figure 1.1. Trail system concept proposal as a part of urban design implementation plan of the City of Irvine. (*Source:* City of Irvine Horizon Year Policies, 1977, City of Irvine/WMRT.)

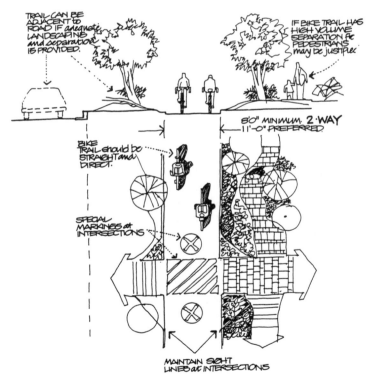

Figure 1.2. An example of guideline pertaining to interaction of automobile, pedestrian, and bikeway. (*Source:* City of Irvine Horizon Year Policies, 1977, City of Irvine/WMRT.)

ARCHITECTURAL FORMS AND DETAILS

Balconies

The incorporation of balconies onto or within the building form is encouraged for both practical and aesthetic value. Balconies should be integrated to break up large wall masses, offset floor setbacks, and add human scale to buildings.

Appropriate

Float finish stucco (required).

Simple, clean, bold projections (encouraged).

Balconies which articulate wall surfaces (encouraged).

Ceramic tile accent trim (encouraged).

Painted wood trim (permitted). Rough sawn wood discouraged.

Discretionary:

Use of single pipe rail above low stucco wall (limited).

Inappropriate:

Transparent walls, such as wrought iron or pipe railing (prohibited).

Figure 1.3. Guidelines pertaining to architectural forms and details best representation of "Franchised Architecture." (*Source:* West Park Design Guidelines, 1985, Irvine Company.)

Planning Area 14" that describe precisely the standards to be met, "The Westpark builders are required to read and follow these guidelines (Figures 1.3 and 1.4). In addition, it is recommended that they review the slide presentation available for viewing at the Irvine Community Development Company."[2] Gaining approval for a project in Westpark is complicated. The Irvine Company has to select a firm as a builder/developer before that firm can begin the process of gaining approval for its development plans. Thus the company has not only formulated the rules, but also chooses those who will operate within them in an attempt to receive the commission for a project.

Exterior Stairs

Simple, clean bold projections of stairways are encouraged to complement the architectural massing and form of a building.   Stairways shall be of float finish stucco with accent trim of complementary colors.

Appropriate

Side walls of smooth or float finish stucco (encouraged).

Accent trim cap or banding of tile (encouraged).

Stairway design and location to complement building form (encouraged).

Innappropriate

Prefabricated metal stairs (prohibited).

Open railings (prohibited).

Figure 1.4. Guidelines pertaining to exterior stairs is another example of "Franchised Architecture." (*Source:* West Park Design Guidelines, 1985, Irvine Company.)

Let us suppose that a developer has passed the first hurdle and is now an accepted firm. Next, the company will furnish the background material needed to prepare a concept plan for the project, and the developer's architect must then prepare the detailed concept plan the company requires. The Irvine Company's Project Review Team and the Urban Planning and Design Department must review and approve the concept plan and authorize the developer (in writing) to submit the plan to the city. This is a joint process between city officials and the major developer. Most review processes were formulated as a safeguard against unchecked building by developers. Further study into the reality of Irvine is needed to determine whose interests are being served.

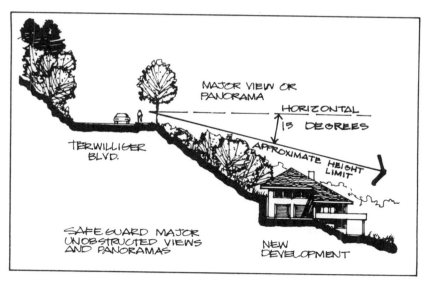

Figure 1.5. An example of design guidelines for height and setback in Terwilliger Parkway. (*Source:* Terwilliger Parkway Design Guidelines, 1983, City of Portland.)

Portland

The Portland (Oregon) City Council sets the stage for cooperation in the "Terwilliger Parkway Design Guidelines" (Figure 1.5).

> Project designers are strongly encouraged to request an early briefing with the Design Commission or their staff prior to formal application for Design Review. Such meetings provide an opportunity for informal discussion of the specific circumstances of the project and how the standards might affect its development.[3]

The architect whose project will have great impact on either its surroundings and/or certain other discretionary aspects must participate in a preapplication conference. After the city receives the application, it schedules a public hearing so that affected and interested citizens can receive information. Following this hearing, the city may ask for modifications in the architectural design proposal. Projects with less impact are eligible for approval by the planning director with or without a public hearing.

The architect for a major project has to submit considerably detailed plans for the early design evaluation process in Portland. In addition to site and landscaping plans, building elevations and a parking plan are necessary.

For visualization of the project, the architect must furnish (1) "large scale plans . . . of the first 25 feet above street level, showing all grade changes and indicating the uses of the various spaces [and (2)] typical floor plans as necessary to describe all levels of the building."[4] The city requires that the architect include a description of the way "the proposed design meets each of the applicable Design Guidelines."[5]

Minneapolis

The situation is very different in Minneapolis, Minnesota. Here the city "can adopt offensive rather than defensive strategies" with their planning and urban design mechanisms. This is true even though "city government . . . has been, in the mayor's words, 'a crazy structure;' i.e., it is a 'weak mayor/strong council' system with a bewildering array of responsibilities and departments.[6] Despite this "crazy structure," the city has a handle on public architecture and urban design evaluation. Some reviews require approval before a project can proceed; others are advisory only.

Concept Plan Review is required for cluster home developments and for apartment developments of ten or more dwelling units. The City Planning Commission is to review:

> All site plans an elevations for cluster developments . . . to ensure a satisfactory relationship of the proposed development with the site and to determine if the character . . . is compatible with the character of the surrounding neighborhood. The city planning commission may reject the proposal for cause or may require alterations in the plan and/or elevations to assure compatibility.[7]

Baltimore

Baltimore, Maryland, has been conducting urban design evaluations long enough for their planning staff to realize the consequences of the approach. As early as 1977, Sydney Brower, then chief of design analysis, Baltimore City Department of Planning, stated:

> Our experience in Baltimore has been that when the situation was bad, design review has been a safeguard against the worst excesses of incompetence. When conditions were favorable, the review process has made for more informed and demanding clients. It has made agency personnel more sensitive to their programming and architectural selection procedures. It has also represented an organized and directed attempt to achieve quality project design and improve the appearance of the sections of the city in which the projects are located.[8]

The Design Advisory Panel reviews "all development plans in the City of Baltimore and . . . advise[s] the architect and his client on functional and aesthetic matters." Prior to this review, and depending on the nature of the project, the "appropriate" real estate officer, project planner, or program manager reviews plans for urban renewal.[9] It is the responsibility of the chief of current planning to look at all other projects first. The Architectural Review Panel evaluates design in the downtown. Since a private, nonprofit corporation took over the development of the harbor area in Baltimore, the Charles Center Review Board (and/or the Historical and Architectural Preservation Board, if appropriate) review(s) certain aspects of projects. Baltimore, too, suggests prereview conferences.

Dallas

At present, Dallas, Texas, has an urban design coordinator with a staff of five to review projects and prepare recommendations to the City Plan Commission and the Board of Adjustment on design matters (in addition to other responsibilities). The level of evaluation varies "from staff review and comment on many of these projects to staff prepared concept plans and design recommendation on others."[10] Dallas also has an Urban Design Task Force, a citizen group appointed by the city manager for advice and counsel to the staff from the consumers' point of view.

For Planned Development Districts, Dallas's Zoning Code (Section 51-4.702) requires a preapplication conference, site plan procedure and analysis, conceptual and development plan, and schedule of construction. Additionally, in certain industrial zoning districts and industrial subdistricts in the Oak Lawn Special Purpose District, there is a Development Impact Review, described as "an administrative procedure that is necessary prior to obtaining a building permit for development considered likely to significantly impact surrounding land uses and infrastructure needs and demands."[11]

The draft of amendments to the ordinance establishing Planned Development District No. 178, the Near Eastside Area, establishes a policy of conformity within conceptual guidelines by providing for a

> preapplication conference. A person desiring to develop property in this district should consult with the director [of planning] to discuss whether the project is consistent with the Near Eastside Conceptual Plan and the requirements of this ordinance.[12]

The director is to examine all Near Eastside projects carefully since they must "score at least 65 points for the primary side [of the project] and at least 50 points for any second side on a design standards test with prohibitions."[13] Points may be awarded for public art or streetscape improvements, elimination of front yard setback, tree plantings, awnings and arcades, use of recommended building materials on the facade (stone, brick, glass block, tile, and cast metal), increased openings (up to 70 percent of total facade area) for doors and windows, and retail usage on the first floor or in the basement.

Indianapolis

In Indianapolis, Indiana, *The City County General Ordinance No. 13* of Marion County and Indianapolis (1983) provides that within the Regional Center and North Meridian Street Corridor additional standards and requirements for use and development shall apply. Following a listing of usual site plan requirements, the ordinance states that the

> details of such a development, including use, signage, building facade treatment, street furnishings and landscaping within the right-of-way, landscape treatment on the site, development intensity, and massing of structure shall be so designed to: . . . (3) create and maintain a desirable, efficient and economical use of land with high functional and aesthetic value, attractiveness and compatibility of land uses within the REGIONAL CENTER, THE NORTH MERIDIAN CORRIDOR, applicable ZONING DISTRICT and with adjacent uses.[14]

Substantive aspects such as these are not easily assessed through process oriented design review guidelines and, therefore, are questionable.

The applicant must seek the approval of the administrator of the Division of Planning of the Department of Metropolitan Development for all development plans by filing a site and development plan. In turn, the zoning administrator may "either approve, disapprove, or approve subject to any conditions, amendments, comments or covenants by the petitioner, the proposed use, site and development plan." Note this final provision: "Public and individual notice of such filing and action by the Administrator shall not be required."[15] The applicant may appeal the administrator's ruling to the Metropolitan Development Commission. The "Regional Center Review Form" includes a section for department of planning contact with neighborhood or business organizations.

Indianapolis's Historic Preservation Commission has developed guidelines for historic districts, Lockerbie Square Historic Area, for example. Design standards are very detailed for renovation, new construction, site development and landscaping, demolition, moving of buildings, and signage. Yet "the contents of this chapter are guidelines and should not be read as absolute rules."[16]

Lincoln

Unlike the previous cities, Lincoln, Nebraska's, urban design guidelines apply only to public improvements or private improvements on public property. Their procedures have been carefully formulated. All seven members of the Urban Design Committee (appointed by the mayor) must be "competent in matters of design, representative of the community, and should include individuals with a demonstrated interest or education in matters of urban design."[17]

There are limits on the committee's powers, however. They may review only those city capital improvements that are "visually significant," public projects "financed by the city of Lincoln or a project in which the city has made or will make some financial contribution . . . when such project affects urban design and aesthetics," or private projects; i.e., those not described above "that will or are proposed to be partially or wholly located on city right-of-way or other city property."[18]

The code provides for two initial evaluations of such projects: "A pre-design conference with the department director or project director [and] when the proposed plans have been prepared." In the case of private projects (as described above), "the prospective applicant and the applicant's architect are entitled to meet with the committee chair." Final review of the concept plans of both public and private projects includes "review of various aspects of design with specific emphasis on the applicable objectives" for submission.[19]

If the Urban Design Committee does not approve of a project, they must "specify in writing the conditions under which a majority of the committee would approve the proposal." Their findings, however, are advisory only. Therefore, "the findings of the committee shall not prevent the implementation of a proposal or be binding on the affected board, department or authority."[20] Approval also may come part by part. Therein lies the lack of consistency of design in Lincoln which can be seen as a problem. However, the freedom provided is great, and the jurisdiction of the review body is not inflated.

Kansas City

Though Kansas City, Missouri, does not have a city-wide formal design evaluation process, design guidelines have been in place since 1978. The first section of the 1979 guidebook dealt with neighborhood preservation and detailed ideas on improving security and privacy, retaining neighborhood shopping and services, and increasing the livability of a neighborhood. Other sections covered major streets and centers, landscape, and buildings. A later guidebook presented architectural preservation and rehabilitation recommendations for homeowners, seeking to serve as inspiration and education. "River City Rehab: Recognizing Your Architectural Assets" "concentrates . . . on particular approaches to help you save the architectural features that give your house its good looks and its market value."[21] These are not very lofty goals for the preservation of buildings. How inspirational and educational are those superficial characteristics which relate only to style?

Responsibility for review of new construction and renovation lies with Kansas City's Building Department and Inspection Division according to the city's building codes and ordinances. Design evaluation may or may not be a part of the discussions with the staff prior to presentation of plans to the planning commission at a formal hearing resulting in approval or disapproval. There is evidence of a desire to expand urban design evaluation. Note that the proposed "Plaza Urban Design and Development Plan" states:

> Projects which are not currently reviewed by the City Development Department and which need only a building permit should be submitted to the City Development Department prior to requesting a building permit. This should be done in order to verify compliance with the planning recommendations and design guidelines of this plan. This review with the City Development Department should occur as early in the design process as possible, preferably during the conceptual design phase.[22]

Other city agencies, such as the Municipal Arts Commission, may have input. The Landmark Commission participates in review of construction in a historic district or of a single historic property. Final approval comes from the city council. Since 1983, the Business Assistance Center, a division of the City Development Department, has aided developers, builders, and their architects through the maze of design criteria, ordinances, and building codes.

In redevelopment projects, the Redevelopment Authority is active in design evaluation with its three-step approval process: concept, schematic, and final. Public discussion is an essential part of the first two steps, and the public also may involve itself in the last phase, which assures that the previously agreed-upon items are included in final drawings.

As an indication of interest in urban design considerations, we might mention the "Downtown Streetscape Manual" updated in 1986. Then, too, urban design evaluation takes place in special districts. For example, there is the Special Review District Main Street with its own Special Review Committee. A 1987 folder, "Special Review District Main Street," outlines the application process (required) and a provision for a preapplication hearing (not required) including the opportunity to "meet with the City Staff about a project [and] make a preliminary presentation to the Special Review Committee." Perhaps admitting to at least some of the special circumstances under which design takes place is an attempt to avoid the generic quality of the guidelines and the built forms which could result.

Another special district is the Board of Trade Urban Renewal Area originally approved in 1980. A modification was proposed in September 1986 (the design review body for "disposition parcels" and development proposals is the Redevelopment Authority):

> Review will evaluate the quality and appropriateness of the proposal on the basis of the design objectives stated in the Plan and in the special land use and building requirements stated in more detailed and refined Development Objectives and Controls which may be prepared for the site.[23]

The formal stages of submission evidence admirable concern on the part of the Redevelopment Authority. For the first stage, Schematic Design, the specifications for the site plan and building plans and sections are kept to a minimum. But the authority is interested in seeing

> all sketches, diagrams and other materials relevant to the proposal which were used by the architect during his initial study and which will help to clarify the architect's problem and his solution to it. . . . [A] written statement [suffices concerning] total square footage, F.A.R., number of parking spaces, structural system and principal building materials, and estimated costs.[24]

San Francisco

San Francisco's urban design and public architecture efforts in California are well known. The city has had an urban design plan since the adoption of a master plan in 1971-1972. The result has been that San Francisco

> became an example of urban renewal at its best; without putting up a penny of cash from its own treasury, San Francisco obtained a quarter of a billion dollars in federal money, in exchange for contributions 'in kind' such as streets and sewers and parks.[25]

Elsewhere, I have described San Francisco as being in the process of institutionalizing urban design.[26] Over the years, the city has tried to develop citizen support for its process of public architecture. Their efforts have been a success or a mixed blessing, depending on where one's interests lie.

> Twice in the Sixties, neighborhood organizations managed to scuttle major freeway projects. . . . Five times in a dozen years, city residents have voted on propositions aimed at braking downtown expansion. One of them, "Prop M" on the November 1983 ballot, sought to put decisive city planning powers into the hands of San Franciscans for Reasonable Growth (SRG), an urban environmental group with ties to ethnic and white-collar neighborhoods alike. It came within 2,000 votes of passing, and developers and city officials took notice.[27]

In October 1985, an ordinance of the City and County of San Francisco, the Downtown Plan, became effective. It soon was clear that for some people its provision did not go far enough in putting a lid on the downtown. Mayor Diane Feinstein herself began to advocate a cap on office development. Her foes—political, environmental, and no-growth advocates—wanted more stringent limits even though "squarish glass and steel boxes, the interchangeable high-rises that dominate skylines across the country, no longer are allowed."[28]

Would including a cap of 950,000 square feet of office space allowed per year for the next three years head off those who wanted even more limits than that? Not likely! San Franciscans soon approved a second Proposition M, a rather complicated measure further limiting office space development downtown. This second Proposition M

> requires that the annual limitation of 950,000 s.f. be reduced to 475,000 s.f. until the total amount of space approved or re-approved since November 19, 1984 is reduced to zero at the rate of 475,000 g.s.f. a year. The total amount of space approved or reapproved is 6,648,979 g.s.f. If all of this space is built, it will take 14 years to reduce that figure to zero.[29]

No wonder, then, that the City Planning Commission did not approve ANY projects proposed for downtown offices during the first year's approval period ending October 26,1986.

Developers want to receive a high rating from the planning staff who evaluate the proposed projects. Many people have input into the decision. The planning staff calls in outside consultants, and the city's Art Commission may review proposals which include public art. In evaluating projects, the planning commission must approve only projects that "promote the public welfare, convenience and necessity."[30] This is a general proviso.

When exemptions and exceptions are needed, Section 309 of San Francisco's code indicates that the approval process for downtown office buildings begins with application for a building permit. This triggers a review process in which many city departments and groups participate. Any one of the participants can stop the application cold in its tracks if problems are found. A public hearing is an early part of this process, a major hurdle to pass because negative feedback might deal a fatal blow to a project, preventing it from going any further. More likely is a request for some modification of plans for the project. Any citizen may request modification to a project at the point when probable approval of that project is announced. Then the commission must call another public hearing; following that comes final approval or disapproval. Developer refusal to carry out modifications requested by the commission results in commission disapproval.

Proposition M has its own priority policies for consistency that the planning commission must heed. For 1986-1987, the planning staff recommended the setting of minimum standards and proposed

> that the Commission consider for approval only projects which score at least 'good' on Criterion B (Master Plan), Criterion C (architectural quality), and Criterion D (Location), and are found to be consistent with the § 101 (Prop. M) priority policies.[31]

We, of course, are most interested in Criterion C, architectural quality. The planning staff was to weigh design quality of the building, of the open space (if applicable), and of the art concept. They were to look for the following characteristics which I have included to illustrate the way in which design evaluation criteria are articulated to the architect or design team:

1. Summary Rating of the Design Quality of the Building:

Excellent: Outstanding qualities of composition and detailing. Few, if any, negative qualities. Building will make an outstanding contribution to the visual quality of the city.

Good: Overall effect is positive although there might be some negative qualities. Building will make a positive contribution to the visual quality of the city. Design responds well to site constraints.

Fair: Possesses neither notable design strengths or weakness, or the positive and negative features tend to cancel each other out. Building will neither add to nor detract from the visual quality of the city.

Poor: Negative qualities clearly dominate the overall effect such as: awkward or graceless composition, excessively bland, dull appearance, poor quality of detailing and/or materials. Building will degrade the visual quality of the city.

2. Design Quality of the Open Space:

Excellent: Accessible, spatially exciting, comfortable open space, providing a variety of experiences and generously fulfilling all the requirements. Represents a most desirable addition to the city's open space.

Good: Features all the necessary elements but in a less generous and exciting manner. Altogether, the space will make a positive contribution to the city's environment.

Fair: Fails to provide some of the elements constituting "useful" open space. Will not particularly be an asset to the city.

Poor: Poorly conceived open space where important elements have been poorly designed or left out. Will detract from the ambience of the city.

3. Quality of the Art Concept:

Excellent: Eminently well placed on the site and successfully integrated with its surroundings, the art work will be highly visible and accessible. The art work(s) in its arrangement makes an outstanding contribution to the city's public spaces.

Good: Works well with its surroundings; is visible and accessible. The choice of location is satisfactory. All in all, the art work(s) is an asset to its surroundings.

Fair: Falls short in certain aspects of placement, scale, or integration with the project; is not as physically and visually accessible as desired. Does not contribute to its surroundings.

Poor: Substantial flaws in location. Poor public visibility and accessibility. Inappropriate scale. Has a negative impact on its surroundings.[32]

Urban design also was to be a factor in judging the suitability of the development for its location.

In evaluating urban design, the following five factors will be considered:

1. *Coherence*
   Does the project contribute to a visually coherent streetscape?
2. *Spatial Definition*
   Does the design contribute to a well proportioned and defined street space for pedestrians?
3. *Scale*
   Does the massing and design detail create a comprehensible building size in relation to adjacent scale of structures?
4. *Context for Preservation*
   Does the building provide a supportive context for noteworthy buildings likely to remain?
5. *Composition in Cityscape*
   Does the building fit into the skyline with grace and harmony?

The evaluation of these five urban design factors will be condensed into a composite evaluation using the following scale:

Excellent: Contributes in significant ways to the quality of streetscape, city views, and positive contextual relationship.

Good: Generally positive in most aspects but not outstanding.

Fair: Little impact of either a positive or negative manner, or good and bad qualities may balance each other out.

Poor: Design would be disruptive to the development of a cohesive streetscape, relates poorly to surrounding buildings, failing to either harmonize or complement.[33]

With three years of experience, the planning staff suggested ways to streamline procedures for evaluation of projects and changed the way the consulting architects are to participate. The new procedure would have the architects reviewing building design along with the staff. Then, later, the architects would submit design graphics to illustrate their opinions as well as short written comments evaluating the projects. The staff prepared new rating charts to make staff comments easily comparable for an overall staff rating.

San Diego

San Diego, California, has a straightforward, layered approach to controlling development and growth while allowing flexibility in requirements. The basis for control is conventional zoning into four main districts (residential, commercial, industrial, and agricultural) with specific permitted uses in each zone. These are the underlying zones; the agricultural zone includes farmland and military usages.[34] The result is a city totally dependent on the automobile as a link among these zones.

Overlaying zones single out areas needing special attention: Height Limitation, Hillside Review, Small Lot, Mobilehome Park, Airport Approach, Sensitive Coastal Resource, Community Plan Implementation, and Institutional. There is a Discretionary Development Permit application procedure when a project does not exactly fit the situation at a proposed location. Community Plans are the implementation element for the city's planning. The "specific precise plans . . . include: (1) goals, (2) objectives, (3) urban design, (4) land use element, (5) transportation element, (6) community facilities element . . . [and] (7) conservation element.[35]

The city first introduced an urban design element during a revision of the General Plan in 1979. Interest in urban design grew out of the contribution of

John Nolen, who in the early part of the century provided a vision for the design and growth of the city; . . . the 1927 General Plan indicates the timelessness of many of the issues addressed in the urban design program [proposed in the mid-eighties].[36]

Are these issues truly timeless or outdated? The city's definition of urban design seems quite practical and realistic:

The General Plan states that Urban Design is a process to foster environmental quality as the city changes. It is the complex interaction of physical and psychological factors relating to our urban environment. Urban design provides the sense of place.[37]

The preciseness of San Diego's approach is worth pondering:

San Diego's proposed Urban Design Program involves refining and clarifying the process by which projects are reviewed. It is not architectural review of every project. It is not requiring public design of private projects. It is not requiring buildings to take on certain architectural styles or certain colors of paint. It is our current system of development processing, including the development regulations found in every zone, and the overlay zones created to deal with certain environmental concerns, such as hillsides and flood plains. It is our Planned District process which was developed to deal with diversity and distinctiveness found in individual neighborhoods.[38]

I have mentioned all these details about zoning, community plans, overlay zones, etc., to indicate the firm commitment to planning from which San Diego logically moved into urban design evaluation. Down through the years, San Diego had finely honed a set of realistic planning procedures. Then in 1974, Kevin Lynch and Donald Appleyard "warned San Diego that its 'paradise' could vanish if new policies were not pursued."[39]

Ripples from their 51-page "Temporary Paradise? A Look at the Special Landscape of the San Diego Region" are still being felt. An outgrowth was the Centre City San Diego Community Plan Urban Design Program adopted by the city council in October 1983, the addition of an urban designer to the planning staff in 1984, and a proposal for a city-wide urban design plan in 1985. The guiding principle for the Centre City Urban Design Program is "to fit proposed projects into the context of existing and proposed development of Centre City."[40]

The Urban Design Program Update, dated December 4, 1987, makes interesting reading, too. One statement stands out: " . . . Urban Design is the ongoing process in which we are presently engaged." What was the state of urban design in 1987?

The Urban Design Program is part of the implementation of all community plans and precise plans. It includes urban design review of city projects, which is currently accomplished but needs to be intensified. It includes amendments to development criteria and creations of new legislation to implement urban design policy. It also includes development of projects and programs addressing transportation, a primary determinant of City form.[41]

Ahead and in progress is a city-wide review of parking regulations.

Seattle

Seattle, Washington, has had a city-wide design commission since 1968. Its main responsibility is to make design suggestions on the city's capital improvements. The recommendations come at three levels in the approval

process: at selection of a consultant, prior to project design as design principles are being set, and periodically as the project progresses to check on
adherence to agreed-upon designs. However, the design commission findings
are not binding on the city council.

Perusal of "Suggestions for Presentation to the Design Commission," a
four-page document, should convince any developer or architect of the necessity to pay attention to design details. In the predesign conference, the commission sets recommended aesthetic, environmental, and design approaches.
That is just the beginning! Still to come are schematic design, design development, construction drawings, and possible resubmittal(s) with changes at any
step. Each of the special districts in Seattle, many with a historic preservation
orientation, has its own design review board and commission. One of the
most interesting and somewhat unusual of the districts is Pioneer Square
Preservation District. Here the motive was to preserve a number of late
nineteenth-century commercial buildings.

A city ordinance has established Pioneer's Review Board to evaluate all
development and renovation in the district; all of its actions are fully set forth
in the ordinances. Its power is limited to making suggestions to the director of
community development. The board participates in the hearing required for
application for a Certificate of Approval and in concept design approval.

The city-wide Landmark Preservation Board has much more power and
can approve or disapprove of design changes proposed for historic sites and
buildings. This board has set development and design review guidelines for
historic districts that became "rules" when filed with the city clerk. Ordinance
109388 (Section 6) establishing the Harvard Belmont Landmark District also
established an Application Review Committee to "review and make recommendations to the Landmark Board for issuance or denial of applications for
Certificates of Approval within the District."[42] "Significant changes" trigger
the need for a Certificate of Approval from the Landmark Preservation Board

> prior to the issuance of any city building, demolition, street use, or other
> permits for proposed work which is within or visible from a public street, alley or
> way, and which involves:
>
> (a) the demolition of, or exterior alterations or additions to, any building
>   or structure;
> (b) any new construction;
> (c) the addition or removal of major landscape and site elements, such as
>   retaining walls, gateways, trees, or driveways.[43]

Even when a building permit is not required "for proposed removal or
addition of significant landscape and site elements,"[44] the applicant still needs
a Certificate of Approval.

An additional indication of a reasonable design evaluation in Seattle is the process for weighing public benefit features in downtown zones. Eligible for consideration are 20 general public benefit features and seven special public benefit features. Acceptance of the special features, ranging from shopping atriums, rooftop gardens, and sculptured building tops to urban plazas and public atriums, will qualify the developer for space bonuses. Review may take place at the same time a Master Use Permit is under consideration or before.

Vail

In the mid-seventies the people of Vail, Colorado, realized that they needed to regulate development and alterations to existing buildings if they were to retain the atmosphere that attracts thousands to Vail, winter and summer. When they began to assess their situation, they discovered that Vail was not the Swiss alpine village look-alike they thought they had, but rather an interesting mix of styles. They established a design review board and addressed "submittal requirements, minimum landscape standards, and appropriate materials for construction" in all of Vail.[45]

Yet it is unclear whether this diversity which has developed will be encouraged or discouraged in favor of an artificial Swiss alpine village. There is always the danger in a tourist-oriented economy of losing the qualities which make it a town. Such a resort town deals in fantasy and illusion. Vail, too, is in danger of becoming a ski amusement park, yet its population of "locals" is quite substantial.

Since the realization of its fragmented nature, the town has completed design guidelines for two specific areas, Vail Village and Vail Lionshead, a secondary downtown area. These guidelines go beyond specifying procedures for developers and homeowners to suggest public and private improvements that need to be made. In 1986, the town undertook the Vail Village Study in an effort to expand the area to which the Vail Village Design Guidelines would apply.

> The plan identifies areas with infill potential, identifies public improvements that would be desired in the study area, and establishes goals and policies for the village that center in large part on development issues.[46]

It is useful to discuss design evaluation in Vail Village because of the sensitive nature of the village and the detailed review process that has been put in place in response.

> The staff has been successful in holding pre-development conferences with developers prior to any significant design work being done. At this meeting, the

staff outlines the review process and, more importantly, identifies issues that may be critical to the proposed development. Given the subjective nature of design criteria, this initial exchange is considered particularly important.[47]

Staff and architect meet informally to discuss the project and its fit with the Vail Urban Design Guide Plan. The Planning and Environmental Commission (PEC) takes over the next step, evaluation of the general form of the project. Next, the staff of the Department of Community Development reviews a submitted proposal "for general compliance with the . . . zoning code" with input from the fire, police, and public works departments prior to the Design Review Board (DRB) conceptual design review. The DRB will determine if "the project generally complies with the design guidelines and [will] forward comments concerning the design to the applicant." Unless the applicant requests it, no vote is taken by the Design Review Board.[48]

The town recommends a conceptual design review "mainly for those applications of a higher impact than single-family and two-family residences, although projects of that nature shall not be excluded the opportunity to request a conceptual design review."[49] Approval by the environmental commission may be a part of the conceptual review.

Underlying Premises of the Guidelines

Our discussion makes it immediately apparent that an extreme amount of energy has been brought to the development of these guidelines. It is also quite obvious that the critical issue in analyzing the varied methods is the underlying premises of the guidelines which have many similarities. Are these cities trying to encourage a more pluralistic environment, a more democratic city? Or have their seemingly objective methods made the process simply a bureaucratic exercise which, through its institutionalization of these objectives, has become quite one-sided and ultimately subjective?

From the mistakes of the Modern movement we have learned that while the functional requirements are of utmost importance, the quality of the built environment does not reside simply in their fulfillment. The less tangible and quantifiable aspects of design also must be explored if architecture is to be meaningful to its users. While many cities mention their concern about aesthetics in the urban environment, the notion is often measured in relation to the compatibility or the fit of the proposed design with the surrounding context.

San Francisco uses language like "successfully integrated with its surroundings" and "fits into the skyline with grace and harmony" to describe the "excellent" building according to its criteria. Indianapolis calls for a "high functional and aesthetic value, attractiveness and compatibility" for the North

Meridian Corridor; Minneapolis, through its guidelines, tries to ensure that the proposed development is "compatible with the character of the surrounding neighborhood."

While these cities define the proper relationship between aesthetic quality and compliance, other cities go further in advising the architect on these matters. Many cities such as Dallas call for projects to be consistent with a conceptual plan determined by the city. Where do the requirements of these plans come from? Are these decisions being made by qualified individuals or bureaucrats? The architect is put in an awkward position. While he or she has been educated in matters of function and aesthetics, now it is the policy makers who advise how to use this education. This is apparent in Seattle and in Baltimore, where an advisory panel guides the architect in "functional and aesthetic matters."

Architects must struggle between personal vision and public policy; as a concerned urbanist, the architect

> must envisage the pressure he wishes to exert on technological progress in terms of his own vision of the most desirable future for the city . . . [yet avoid the] problem of the urbanist as an elite specialist opposed to the operation of the general will.[50]

He or she also is forced to communicate on a level not conducive to the communication of design ideas. In Portland, for example, the architect is required to submit written descriptions, verbal justifications of visual and spatial ideas.

This "modern mentality, . . . which is represented by the rationality of industry and bureaucracies, reinforces the pressure on architects to explain their ideas in matter-of-fact terms."[51] We have turned these intangible issues of architecture into simply another functional requirement. While educated in craft, the architect's role is diminished to that of service. By using "objectively verifiable knowledge" as the criterion for the integrity of design, we then subject aesthetic concerns to the same models of judgment as apply to "pragmatic considerations."[52] It is essential to recognize that farsighted leadership from enlightened planners and architects must combine with effective communication of the benefits of public architecture to the developers, the government, and the citizens. Practically speaking, that is what keeps the city alive, vibrant, and healthy—and architects and planners employed.

The bureaucracy involved is evident in the layering of process which results in complicated, and at times quite intense, procedures for obtaining approval of an architectural concept. The process has proliferated to an extreme level, a machine that focuses on keeping everything under control. Perhaps it even keeps creativity and innovation in check. These layers of process require a great deal of study and experience by the architect to be able to move through them freely. As we see in Kansas City, the web of procedures and policies is so tangled that an additional agency must step in to guide those who participate in the process. In essence, the rules of the game and the arena in which it is to be played become more important than the game itself, which in this case is the creative process of architecture of the city.

At the early stages of developing an urban project, the developers' understanding of the milieu of the city, as well as their knowledge of the architecture and design mechanisms they must observe, are both of importance. They must do a great deal of homework—and rely on the knowledge of the architect-designer—so that their projects will be financially viable and will not be in controversy from the onset. However, much of this homework is done in the area of restrictions and compliance mechanisms that may create obstacles for the project rather than in the areas that exert positive influence on a project. The result can be a generic design package that may overcome the bureaucratic hurdles while ignoring the true nature of its urban context, "a franchise commodity to development pressures."[53]

One might think that the fierce competition for approval of office projects which Proposition M has created will further aid San Francisco's urban design efforts. However, it stands to reason that developers will be more cooperative about strict adherence to the code and ordinances, and there will be less grousing about design guidelines as well. Thus, this fierce competition seems only to encourage conformity, reinforcing guidelines, but at what cost to creativity and innovation? Pierluigi Nicolin explains this tendency.

> Any architecture whose basic constitution is formed by totally internal, typological, formal, and constructive laws will tend to impose itself as a practice which those involved do no more than accept.[54]

In the process of architectural concept evaluation, the evaluator's most important concern becomes the definition of the context within which the proposed building is to be located and the building's appropriateness to this context, seeking compatibility with the immediate context instead of engaging in analysis beyond the immediately defined boundaries of the site.[55] The way in which a city chooses to deal with diversity and distinctiveness is something to consider. San Diego is perhaps one of the few cities in the United States that is dealing with architecture of the city in an inductive way rather than a deductive way, focusing on the premise of the existing city and its future rather than looking to the past to create its present.

1.2 ENVIRONMENTAL IMPACT

In 1985, I called attention to a lack of sufficient concern for environmental matters in many American cities, citing as one of the principal reasons that "planning studies, even when they attempt to incorporate environmental factors, focus inappropriately on the natural environment rather than on the relationship between the built and natural environments."[56] In other words, I felt that cities did not undertake an urban design approach toward preservation/enhancement of natural factors. They did not ask how the inevitable development will affect the environment and how the environment may be expected to affect the development and the city appropriately. I, likewise, expressed a concern that "the role of natural processes in urban design/planning will continue to be underestimated."[57]

How well are the cities we are examining doing in protecting and enhancing the natural environment? Are they integrating environmental concerns with public architecture? In doing so, are they looking at the ecological phenomena of the total built environment? Our task will be difficult because many of the cities have but an ad hoc approach to environmental assessment. Searching through the zoning code, ordinances, and design evaluation procedures (assuming that the latter exists!) may not provide much of a clue to the city's concern for environmental matters. This by itself may illustrate the level of superficiality with which the cities are dealing with this important category.

Vail

Let us begin our study with Vail, a town that owes a great deal of its attractiveness to the natural context and stands to lose its appeal if environment is ignored or misused as development inevitably occurs. It seems superfluous to observe that the charm of Vail is its setting: the backdrop of mountains; the crisp, clear air; the unspoiled natural surroundings so close to the built-up areas that have attempted to maintain the aura of villages, an aura that is growing more artificial. Yet how quickly all this could be spoiled: the mountains no longer visible from villages that have not thought about maintaining vistas, the air polluted, and the surroundings filled with sprawling growth.

Because Vail's aesthetic quality forms a significant contrast, the town has taken on the task of protecting its assets. The Purpose of Vail's *Zoning Title* (zoning code) includes several specific references to environmental concerns:

1. to provide for adequate light, air, sanitation, drainage, and public facilities;
2. to secure safety from fire, panic, flood, avalanche, accumulation of snow, and other dangerous conditions; . . .
7. to prevent excessive population densities and overcrowding of the land with structures;
8. to safeguard and enhance the appearance of the town;

9. to conserve and protect wildlife, streams, woods, hillsides, and other desirable natural features;

10. to assure adequate open space . . . [58]

When the "Design Guidelines" became a part of the *Zoning Title,* their intent included references to design evaluation as essential to environmental protection. "In order to preserve the natural beauty of the town and its setting, . . . the improvement and alteration of open space . . . shall be subject to design review as specified in this Chapter." Then follow "the objectives of design review" including:

C. to prevent the unnecessary destruction or blighting of the natural landscape; . . .

E. to protect neighboring property owners and users by making sure that reasonable provision has been made for such matters as . . . surface water drainage, sound and sight buffers, the preservation of light and air, and those aspects of design not adequately covered by other regulations which may have substantial effects on neighboring land uses . . . [59]

Unless the zoning administrator determines that it is not necessary, preliminary/final design evaluation must include a topographic survey with

existing trees or groups of trees having trunks with diameters of four inches or more, . . . rock outcroppings and other significant natural features such as avalanche areas, one hundred year flood plain, and slopes of forty per cent or more . . .

Item (c) of the same section deals with drainage plans: "For all developments this study shall include a contour map . . ." Going on to item (i), we find regulations for the erosion control and revegetation required in all developments of two or more acres and which may be required in smaller developments "based upon conditions of slope and soil stability."[60] Soils and climate are factors for an architect to consider when selecting materials for landscaping. Vegetation should consist of plants "indigenous to the Rocky Mountain alpine and sub-alpine zones or . . . capable of being introduced into these zones."[61] Section .051.E of 18.54 deals with park design guidelines and covers such elements as preservation of "open meadows of native grasses and flowers, and permanent stands of evergreens; site revegetation . . . [and] erosion control."[62] For preservation of vistas, Vail has established a View Corridor Map on which the most significant view corridors and focal points are indicated. The aim is to protect the views from major pedestrian areas or public plazas. Views are important in and of themselves, but they also are reference points with which visitors can orient themselves and determine their location in the Village. The Design Review Board examines projects to determine that they do not block view corridors or the view from any pedestrian areas.

Sun access and shading are of concern because of Vail's alpine climate; even in the summer, it can be uncomfortably cool in the shade. Therefore, "new or expanded buildings should not substantially increase the spring and fall shadow pattern (March 21 through September 23) on adjacent properties or the public R.O.W. [right of way]."[63] Building height and massing are examined because of possible shading, as are decks and patios. The design considerations for the latter suggest "direct sunlight from 11:00–3:00 to increase use by many days a year and to protect from wind."[64]

The 1986 "Vail Land Use Plan" (for the entire town) spoke to environmental issues:

> New subdivisions should not be permitted in high geologic hazard areas (1.7).
> Recreational and public facility development on National Forest lands may be permitted where no high hazards exist [under certain nonenvironmental conditions] (1.8). . . .
> Vail should accommodate most of the additional growth in existing developed areas (infill areas) (1.12).[65]

Development pressures in Vail are strong enough that framers of the 1986 plan felt it necessary to specify constraints on areas for development including floodplains, river corridors, and bodies of water; slopes steeper than 40 percent; rockfall, debris flow, and debris and snow avalanche areas; and open space and parklands. Further, in an attempt to anticipate problems, there was examination of similar hazards in nearby national forest land, areas with potential for annexation to the town. The Task Force analyzed parcels with a less than 40 percent slope and added them to the plan area. As a general proviso, the "Land Use Plan" states that "the quality of the environment should be protected as the Town grows."[66]

California Environmental Quality Act of 1970

California cities and towns must include environmental monitoring for all development in their jurisdictions because of the California Environmental Quality Act of 1970 (CEQA). Amendments since then have refined its provisions: Municipalities must follow CEQA unless they have enacted environmental protection ordinances of their own. As we consider environmental controls in Irvine, San Francisco, and San Diego, we will come to understand the impact of CEQA in California.

Irvine

The Irvine Company and the State of California have enabled Irvine to retain many of the attractive natural features of Orange County. Additionally, the City of Irvine has sustained tight controls. Growing even faster than was anticipated when the first plans were laid in 1959, Irvine became the fastest growing city in California between 1970 and 1980.

The City of Irvine is a mixture of land uses and contains a number of planned communities. Irvine's open space occurs as spines branching off the central activity corridor, city parks, and agricultural land. Main roads circle the villages, and pedestrian and bicycle paths and landscaped buffers keep traffic and its pollution out of residential areas. Proposition 13 has slowed down some of the plans for landscaping, trail systems, the development of Peters Canyon Wash for passive recreation, and other amenities. However, some of the villages have private parks that are collectively financed.

Many types of projects in Irvine require approval of a Landscape Construction Plan as a part of the evaluation procedure: owner maintained residential; commercial, industrial, and institutional; city projects on city owned or maintained properties; and association maintained development, redevelopment, and rehabilitation. If an irrigation system is used, there must be pressure loss calculations. A soils report is another requirement in order to alert the architect to planting conditions, important because of maintenance and mandated replacement costs and erosion control measures.

Environmental impact evaluation is required for all development. If a project is large or greatly affects the environment, a presubmission meeting with the Department of Community Development (DCD) usually takes place. After weighing the Environmental Application, the DCD decides whether or not the developer must file an Environmental Impact Report (EIR). The application asks for information on plant and tree cover, watercourses and drainage, slopes and soils, and paleontological, archaeological, and historical data. An Environmental Analysis/Initial Study requires information on air, earth and biological resources, noise, and light and glare. The DCD may need additional information such as that supplied by an Acoustical Report Information Sheet.

A Negative Declaration by the DCD indicates that a project will not have major effect on the environment. The DCD or a consultant will prepare an EIR for all other projects, with cost borne by the developer. Guidelines in the Environmental Evaluation for Subsequent Activity under a Program EIR leads the DCD through an EIR, making sure that all environmental impacts have been considered. Also involved is public review and an opportunity for the public to appeal DCD environmental decisions, Negative Declarations as well as EIRs.

Completion of the Irvine Master Environmental Assessment in 1986 has made the work of DCD much easier; now the department's staff have authoritative information at their fingertips. The assessment includes complete data on and maps of all environmental constraints and baseline data maps on related environmental matters. Two indices give information on environmental documents and an archaeological survey. When all this data is computerized, the city will have an even more valuable tool because the information will be more readily accessible. In addition, Irvine encourages the use of solar energy as another way to cut pollution.

San Diego

In response to the need to monitor environmental quality, San Diego has recently adopted a Resource Protection Overlay Zone (RPOZ) ordinance requiring a Resource Protection Permit covering concerns about wetlands, floodways, floodplain fringes, and hillsides. Applicants for building permits in affected areas must satisfy these environmental requirements before initiating other steps in the permit process. A preliminary consultation will establish whether or not an RPOZ permit is required. Then, an RPOZ application, as well as the initial environmental study required by CEQA, will be filed.

As in Irvine, a Negative Declaration may be possible. Reviews by the Subdivision Review Committee and certification of conformation by the Environmental Quality Division of the Planning Department and a public hearing then follows. At the public hearing, the planning director reports on evidence (from a field examination, planning department analyses, and reports from other city departments) that the project will have minimal impact on

> sensitive natural resources and environmentally sensitive areas . . . [and on] sensitive habitats and scenic resources in adjacent parks and recreation areas . . . [with] adequate buffer areas to protect such resources; . . . [this] will minimize the alterations of natural landforms and will not result in undue risks from geological and erosional forces and/or flood and fire hazards.[67]

The planning director issues a Resource Protection Permit when all environmental issues appear to have been satisfied. The permit may include special conditions specific to the nature of a particular area. In addition to its work on RPOZ matters, the Environmental Quality Division in the Planning Department plays a vital role in the city's general conformance to CEQA requirements.

It would seem appropriate to comment on some of San Diego's other environmental efforts at this point. Consider the *Mid-City Community Plan,* for example. First of all, CEQA "requires that environmental impact reports be prepared for all community plans [and] separate, detailed EIR's . . . for all significant projects, including those implementing the Plan."[68] The plan also had to take into account the Regional Air Quality Strategy to help meet air quality standards of the National Clean Air Act. The plan notes a "lack of available land and resources" with regard to remedying a deficiency in park acreage and recommends "creative solutions."[69] And later, "existing zoning provides only minimal potential for preserving open space."[70] What does exist is already identified in the City of San Diego *Progress Guide and General Plan,* Open Space Element. Also noted are some undesignated steep slopes and undeveloped canyons.

The Urban Design Element of the *Mid-City Community Plan* includes objectives addressing landscaping, usable open space, and better conditions for pedestrians and cyclists. The plan specifically mentions the need to consider maintenance costs in the selection of vegetation for landscaping, minimization of effects of development on sensitive areas, and encouragement of water and energy conservation by means of appropriate design and landscaping techniques. To accomplish the last suggestion, the plan proposes additional landscaping to lessen effects of high density and increase shade and visual screening, use of drought-resistant plantings, siting and design of structures to take advantage of shading and breezes, and utilization of solar heating and cooling with adequate insulation. To prevent erosion and retain natural slopes, developers should make provision for retaining soil displaced by construction, restore natural contours using ground cover there and on all "manufactured slopes."[71]

In discussing urban design criteria, the *Mid-City Community Plan* kept its emphasis on environmental amelioration.

1. Don't site very tall buildings next to low ones. The result can be "excessive shadows [and] undesirable wind tunnels. . . ."[72]
2. Where possible, provide a "usable courtyard, roof top, or other recreation area [and incorporate] recreational amenities and ample landscaping."[73]

The *Mid-City Community Plan* also "recommended that the open space system along the south rim of Mission Valley be given highest priority for acquisition because of its extremely high visibility." Likewise it suggested the use of transferable development rights as a means of protecting open space and gaining funds for Mid-City. It mentioned protection of privately owned slopes and canyon systems as "among the few remaining wildlife habitats within the urbanized area of the city [and proposed allowing] access for study and passive recreation" only.[74] In special neighborhood plans (e.g., Normal Heights), a 1987 amendment of the plan reiterates protection of canyons, creation of new parks, and improvement of existing parks and playgrounds.[75] In Kensington and Talmadge, the amendment seeks to preserve open space by "environmental constraints, clustering of development with minimum grading, and generally limiting the development of slopes." Adequate access to the canyons and other high-risk areas will help with fire control in Kensington and Talmadge.[76]

The *Mid-City Design Plan* is an appendix to the *Mid-City Community Plan* and details urban design responses to positions taken and to recommendations in the main plan. For example, there are specific landscaping, energy, park, open space, and bicycle route suggestions for implementation. In 1986, the city council passed a city-wide landscaping ordinance which is administered by a landscape ordinance planner. This ordinance will help to coordinate landscaping in the various neighborhood and overlay zones so that continuity will result.

San Francisco

In San Francisco it is the Office of Environmental Review (OER) that makes a decision about necessity for an EIR. If the OER finds that a project has but a small environmental impact, it turns the application over to the planning director for the issuance of a Negative Declaration. However, the OER may call for an Environmental Evaluation (EE). Should this EE reveal minimal impact, then again, the planning director becomes immediately involved. Should there be clear environmental impact, then a full-scale EIR is prepared to guide the architect in meeting environmental standards.

CEQA requires public notice of the issuance of a Negative Declaration. If after ten days no citizen appeals the decision, the Negative Declaration becomes final. An appeal results in a call for an EIR, or the OER may ask the architect to alter his project and mitigate the environmental effects according to the concerns evidenced in the EIR. As before, all this precedes any applications for other permits or design evaluation.

In response to CEQA, the *Master Plan of the City and County of San Francisco* outlines the following elements.

1. Conserving San Francisco's natural resources (as specified by CEQA: "Waters of the Bay and Ocean, fish and other marine animals, the shoreline, air, fresh water for consumption and for fire fighting, land, plants, and animals of the city's land area and lakes") (9.2)
2. Landscaping

3. Reducing pollution and noise
4. Emphasizing conservation of energy and use of alternate energy sources
5. Protecting land resources by avoiding landslides and erosion

Portland

In the 1970s, Portland became acutely aware that both the natural context of the Portland area and the presence of vacant land were causing development pressures. The Willamette riverfront in Portland had deteriorated, partly because of decline in the lumber industry. If ever a time had come for Portland to protect its assets, this was it.

In 1972, Portland proposed a Transit Mall with park-and-ride centers to encourage bus ridership and cut air pollution, thereby helping to meet federal air quality standards. This was a part of Portland's Downtown Plan, which also provided a ceiling in parking to further cut automobile use and protection of scenic view corridors by establishing maximum building heights—likewise helpful in maintaining sunlight on open spaces.

Though an environmental impact statement is not part of Portland's design evaluation process, and no assessment is required by the state, there are some environmental concerns built into the evaluation of projects. Looking first at the *Downtown Design Guidelines* (1983), we find suggestions "that new public parks and plazas offer frequent opportunities for public use, are oriented to receive sunlight, and integrate well with the downtown pedestrian circulation plan."[77]

To further alternatives to the automobile, the *Downtown Plan Handbook* (1981) recommends support of walking and bicycle use by making trips across bridges safer and by developing bikeways throughout the core with connections to nearby areas. Observing that "the riverfront is one of the few places which provide the city dweller with the opportunity to get in touch with the natural environment," the handbook offers the opinion that it would be well "to make the Willamette River free of pollution and safe for water-oriented activities and marine life."[78] Interestingly, several large grassy areas were to be left as "'meadows' to provide space for unspecified park uses and future flexibility."[79]

The "Application for Design Review" does not require any environmental data, asking only for a site plan with all buildings and land uses within 200 feet indicated. A handout entitled "Historical Landmarks Commission Review Procedure" does specify that the staff shall consult with neighborhood groups and District Advisory Councils concerning a project "depending on the complexity and environmental effect."[80] Then note that the *Zoning Code,* in giving site or development plan requirements, asks for showing "natural features such as watercourses and topography, ... types of vegetation, ... [and] street trees."[81]

Portland's new *Central City Plan* (effective July 1988), which expands the *Downtown Plan* beyond its original borders and reaffirms strong planning policies, states in a section entitled "Purpose and Mission of the Central City Plan" that the plan

> recognizes the unique environmental setting and historic precedence of the area. ... [Specifically, the plan is to] identify additional public amenities that contribute to the urban and natural environment, and to livability for citizens within that environment, assure ... exciting environment and attractions for residents, as well as visitors ... [82]

Amendments to this *Central City Plan* provide "an incentive for the creation of needed open space and efficient use of land."[83] The developer must dedicate space as a public park; he or she also can transfer height requirements from a lot that will become open space to another development lot—with limitations on the total new height allowed.

Seattle

Policy and Procedures for Seattle's Design Commission lays out the commission's responsibilities for environmental evaluations of city development projects. From the predesign conference through design development, the design commission considers environmental concerns parallel with and as part of design evaluation. First, "the commission will formulate recommended aesthetic, environmental design principles and objectives for the project, together with the appropriate City official and the designer."[84]

A part of the next step, schematic design, is "a description of known or anticipated environmental effects." Finally, in design development: "Information relating to environmental impact review requirements should be brought to the attention of the Commission."[85] One of the criteria justifying only limited review is that the project be "small in scope or budget and do[es] not raise serious design or environmental problems."[86] Recall that the findings of the commission are but advisory to the mayor and city council.

Chapter 23.56 of the *Zoning Code* sets the first purpose of Overlay Districts: "To conserve and enhance the City of Seattle's unique natural marine and international setting and its environmental and topographic features. ..." Environmentally sensitive areas are limited to "areas of steep slopes which are: known slide areas identified by documented history; or potential slide areas based on documented geological characteristic. . . ."[87] The other special review boards in Special Districts, Pike Place Market Historical District, Pioneer Square Preservation District (and at least five others) must include in their regulations environmental impact assessments as in the Design Commission procedures because of Washington's *State Environmental Policy Act (SEPA) Rules,* adopted in 1984. According to these rules, Seattle had to develop its own SEPA regulations by October 1984.[88]

In 1985 Seattle undertook an updating of Seattle 2000, calling it "Seattle 2000 Action Inventory: An Inventory of City Actions Related to the Seattle 2000 Goals, 1973-1984." It noted that the city enacted zoning legislation in 1984 that restricts development in certain greenbelts, and it has turned federal surplus land into two major parks. Citizens now can help maintain parks near their homes under the Adopt-a-Park program. In conclusion, the inventory stated:

> There is no one central place in the Land Use Policies or in the City's planning which addresses the preservation of Seattle's assets. However, it is an underlying principle of most of the land use related planning that is being undertaken. Measures to preserve assets are included in the Land Use Policies, the Shorelines Master Program, the Parks Department's proposed Policy Plan and projects and the greenbelt legislation.[89]

Baltimore

In Seattle they call it Adopt-a-Park. In Baltimore the Shape Up Parks program also enlists citizen help through neighborhood and community organizations, volunteering time to clean up parks, recreation centers, playgrounds, and neighborhoods. "Street Tree Planting Standards" is a small pamphlet giving citizens instructions on buying and planting their own trees to complement Baltimore's "vigorous tree planting program."[90] Listed are suitable trees for planting, directions, and an admonition to acquire a tree-planting application from the Bureau of Parks Forestry Division.

The city does encourage citizen participation. Community and neighborhood organizations usually have their own review panels to evaluate all construction and renovation. They are the first line of defense against development that may be harmful to the environment or falls short in some other respect.

"Public access to the waterfront [is] a top priority . . . through building height limits, view corridors and a promenade stretching all the way [from Fells Point] to the Inner Harbor."[91] In the Canton Waterfront Area, restoration has turned old warehouses into commercial and office space, a restaurant, a health club, apartments, and a 365-car garage. Says one of the occupants, "Tindeco seems in harmony with the water, the birds. . . ."[92]

Three of the objectives for the Inner Harbor Project I Renewal Plan pay lip service to environmental concerns:

1. To eliminate unhealthful, unsafe and unsanitary conditions such as the dangers caused by flooding, the causes of noxious fumes or noisome odors . . .
4. To provide land for needed public improvements such as open space, access to the water's edge, active recreation areas, and pedestrian and vehicular circulation.
5. . . . [To establish] adequate circulation, service, light and air to all parcels of the area . . . [93]

However, the "Submission Requirements" handout from the Design Advisory Panel (DAP) does not show any great emphasis on environmental concerns in the panel's design evaluation process. There is an expressed concern for landscape quality.

A plethora of neighborhoods, each distinctive and unique, is one of Baltimore's most interesting assets and the particular concern of the Neighborhood Progress Administration. The 1986 Rand McNally Survey said that Baltimore is "one of America's most liveable cities."[94] How has this happened? The Neighborhood Incentive Program (NIP) has helped. Among other actions, NIP provided matching dollars for a park in the Wilson Park Neighborhood.

Let us close our discussion of Baltimore with a look to the future. "Baltimore's Development Program, 1988–93" details planned capital improvements for that period. Included are:

1. Park and recreation plans: upgrading, rehabilitation, repair, renovation, development of a new park, acquisition of parkland for expansion
2. A major storm water project
3. Wastewater programs "to meet the waste water requirements of future regional growth, while maintaining stringent environmental standards"[95]
4. Water supply programs
5. "Modify or replace electrical transformers or associated equipment containing polychlorinated biphenyl liquids"[96]
6. "Harbor deepening; . . . study to determine the extent of subsurface and surface water contamination from on-site chrome tailing and development of remedial measures [at the Dundalk Marine Terminal; development of] a master plan defining alternatives for the disposal of dredged material from the maintenance of the Baltimore Harbor and channels through the year 2000 and beyond"[97]

Dallas

The final two consultants' reports in the *Dallas Downtown Plan, 1986* for the City of Dallas and the Central Dallas Association responded to central city concerns and dealt "with different aspects of creating a superior environment in downtown Dallas,"[98] but a most intensive environmental concern for the city is development evaluation in floodplain and the White Rock Escarpment areas. The floodplain ordinances apply in federally designated floodplain areas, in those areas later found to be flood prone (some of which may already have their own regulations), and along streams and creeks. The aim of floodplain management is to move storm water naturally, rather than to create expensive man-made channels, and to allow development of filled land "where it would not create other flood problems and where public acquisition is not required for environmental protection or recreation purposes."[99]

Engineering, ecological, and scenic resource criteria are used to establish proper land usage in the floodplain. Ecologic and scenic factors include "maturity and diversity of woodland stands, wildlife habitat potential, . . . finding of some rare or endangered or locally threatened species, . . . unique views, compositional effects, and other visual features.[100] Observance of the engineering criteria should prevent erosion and provide natural drainage areas.

The White Rock "Escarpment Report" has provided Dallas with detailed environmental information on this steep slope/bluff corridor that extends from Sherman, Texas, through Dallas and past San Antonio. Sudden development pressures, expanding opportunities for employment, and the consequent need for expressway links brought the fragility of the escarpment to the attention of design and planning officials.

The original 1977 report was followed by Ordinance 17216 in November 1981. The objectives of this ordinance indicate the all-encompassing protection the city desires to give:

(1) To preserve a unique landscape feature within the city.
(2) To preserve natural habitats for vegetation and wildlife.
(3) To preserve natural features such as rock outcroppings, native plant materials, natural hydrology and areas of visual significance.
(4) To preserve natural moderators of climate.
(5) To preserve the view of and from the escarpment.
(6) To protect against siltation of area streams and lakes. . . .
(7) To minimize costs of public improvements to correct and reduce hazards and pollution.
(8) To minimize the effects of grading and to insure that the natural character of the escarpment is retained.
(9) To provide safety against unstable slopes or slopes subject to erosion and deterioration.

(10) To ensure that development is planned to fit the topography, soils, geology, hydrology, and other conditions existing on the proposed site. . . .[101]

Dallas also has adopted some special-purpose district ordinances which recognize such environmental factors as open space, streetscape, and pedestrian facilities. In the Central Business District (CBD), for example, city participation in pedestrian facilities is through special funds set aside for this purpose and incentives that "encourage CBD developers to do more than merely meeting *minimum* required facility standards."[102]

Lincoln

In 1986, following the Taubman Company's conceptual plan for development in the Lincoln downtown section, the mayor appointed an Ad Hoc Committee on Project Design to review the Taubman plan. After complimenting the company on recommending "generous interior open spaces, . . . exterior open spaces at principal entrances, . . . [and] continuation of the existing street tree plans on all sides of the project, . . . the committee felt strongly that the project was deficient in open space."[103] Recognizing "that this project cannot fulfill all the open space requirements of the central business district," the committee suggested "well defined open space, . . . a major plaza." Additionally, the committee wanted other, smaller open spaces "developed around the whole perimeter of the project, incorporating existing spaces."[104]

The city's Urban Design Committee's comments on the project described the need for providing "Lincoln's civic living room . . . [with] water, shade and sunshine." The committee also expressed hope of continuing an

> advisory role in this important project, with involvement at several critical stages: . . . consultation at schematic phase, review of project agreement, consultation at preliminary design phase [and] . . . at design development phase, [and] final review of design.[105]

Indianapolis

In April 1988, Indianapolis discussed improvement to its existing Sky Exposure Plane Standards for the CBD. The regulations in place for Sky Exposure Plane One permitted "the maximum amount of building floor area to be developed per lot in the CBD," while Plane Two was more "restrictive so as to provide for a greater degree of light and air exposure." Sky Exposure Plane Three provided special development rules for "properties abutting Monument Circle," one of Indianapolis's major open spaces in the CBD.[106]

The changes proposed that buildings be so constructed that parts of the American Legion/World War Memorial Mall and the Indianapolis Water Company Canal, as well as Monument Circle, would be sunlit during the hours of 10:00 A.M. to 2:00 P.M., when there is the most outdoor activity in the CBD. Further, the new Sky Exposure Plane Standards were to expand to cover

> all other areas of the Regional Center Zone in CBD-1, CBD-2, and CBD-3 . . . to ensure that a greater amount of light (not direct sunlight) and air reach street level than would otherwise occur under existing development standards. A secondary result of requiring buildings to step back from public spaces is that more buildings will have a view of that open space and greenspace, giving a greater sense of access to light and air to the occupants of the building.[107]

In the late seventies, Indianapolis set its sights on improving the city with *Indianapolis 1980–2000*, which (among many other things) envisioned a public/private partnership to develop 250 acres into White River Park to the west of downtown, a revitalization of the midtown neighborhood, landscaping of the major open spaces, and a general increase in the ambience of downtown Indianapolis to attract more people to live there. White River Park has been described as a "significant urban form giver" because it helps integrate pedestrian open space throughout the downtown.

> In part, Indianapolis is beginning to achieve a new and rather successful urban form because it can build upon well-designed urban spaces, parks, and estates of the 19th century. Many of these were ignored or forgotten for nearly a half-century or longer as the Indianapolis power structure went through what appears now to have been a populistic, anti-aesthetic drought of design ideas.[108]

"Indianapolis 1980–2000 Regional Center General Plan" (1981) saw a need for more small neighborhood parks. Only fairly recently has Indianapolis accepted federal monies for projects, monies that come with federal regulations and requirements—including, of course, the environmental assessment.

Kansas City

In the *Kansas City Urban Design Guidebook*, first issued in 1978, we can see that Kansas City even then was melding environmental concerns into a complete urban design scheme. "The Urban Design Guidebook outlines ways in which the city's character can be improved through coordination of public and private land development investments, . . . identifies 18 valuable characteristics" in the city and offers suggestions on enhancing them by application of urban design principles.[109] Among many other things, the guidebook promulgates land-scaping as a means of establishing order and vitality and accommodating "ecological processes . . . to reduce costs and produce marketable features."[110]

Have these guidelines been put to good use? Recall that Kansas City must use them informally, so they are not activated automatically. In 1985 the Redevelopment Authority seized an opportunity to make

> an improved aesthetic environment for the downtown area, . . . accomplished in part by a streetscape improvement program that will upgrade the standard of materials and create an orderly system of street furniture and streetscape elements.[111]

Specified are the size and recommended type of trees and detailed planting and replacement instructions including installation of a tree-watering plan.

"A City Plan" echoes the 1978 guidelines by suggesting that Kansas City's waterways be enhanced and made more available for public use and that vistas be created and preserved. Particular attention was paid to the Missouri River downtown by expressing a hope that access could be improved. Additionally, the plan called for protection of "the area within the floodway and floodplain of all rivers within the city's boundaries from erosion of their natural state" except for flood control, which should be handled unobtru-sively.[112] The plan recommended looking for possible natural wildlife sections in these areas.

This revised plan states that the two most important urban design principles are a visually understandable environment and quality of life:

> An attractive physical setting, organized around parks, boulevards, and water-ways, and with quality public facilities and active civic and arts endeavors, enhances quality of life.[113]

The mission statement of "A City Plan for Urban Design and Development Policy," in another forward-looking document, states:

> This planning project will focus primarily on the physical environment and issues of urban design, rather than on social and economic issues. This focus has been selected because physical planning and urban design have not received enough of the city's attention in recent years.[114]

Minneapolis

Consistently, Minneapolis has tried to have environmental matters under control. Consider *State of the City 1983,* for example, which gives the physical environment a section of its own. In "Physical Environment Overview," Minneapolis was able to point to progress in control of Dutch elm disease, in meeting air quality standards, in the handling of hazardous waste, in control of pollution (most complaints in 1983 were for loud stereos and parties), and in raising lake water quality. Budgetary cuts affected tree replacement, but more employee time could be spent in tree trimming because of the easing in Dutch elm disease infestations. Carbon monoxide pollution was less of a problem in the city, partly due to the "designation of Hennepin Avenue and First Avenue North as one way streets."[115]

Further environmental information is available under Property Services.[116] The city reported that the quality of water and the safety standards for monitoring its purity were in good shape. Separation of sanitary and storm sewers reached within 89-90 percent of completion, making possible an eventual lessening of costs for treatment and of pollution from snow melt and storm runoff. Organized recycling has cut the amount of household trash that must be disposed of. Rising energy costs continue as a problem; but the city planned to initiate a number of energy conservation moves, educating the public on conservation and funding conservation retrofits.

Minneapolis maintains an extensive park and recreation system, including a bird sanctuary and a bog area retained in its natural state. The city completed a riverfront plan and a plan for rerouting of Great River Road along the west bank of the Mississippi.

Metro 2000 Plan has been guiding Minneapolis's growth and change for 30 years. The January 1988 update provides policy "guides to the Minneapolis downtown of the year 2000."[117] This latest version heeds earlier commitments:

> Environmental, energy and urban design factors are not "add-on" items to be considered after a "go-ahead" decision has been made. They rank equally with determination of economic demand, current and future costs and financial feasibility.[118]

Minneapolis's government and citizens have taken to heart the statement that "virtually all natural elements . . . will be managed by man. . . ."[119] As early as 1968, the city established CUE, the Committee on Urban Environment, made up of government and citizen representatives committed and dedicated to design excellence and a beautiful urban environment. Active in advisory design evaluation for the city government, CUE also encourages citizen involvement in neighborhood and park cleanup and fix-up and tree planting. CUE also promotes awareness of all sorts of environmental matters.

Beyond Environmental Impact

While the efforts of the 12 case cities to preserve the environment certainly cannot be criticized, the need to further the notion of "environmental" impact beyond its fundamental sense does exist, for environmental impact can go beyond the traditional categories of evaluation. When do the existing urban layers enter into this category of environmental concern? It is necessary to move beyond the reactionary methods. We have learned our lesson well from destruction by urban renewal, yet we must also learn from the mistakes of wholesale preservation of "old" buildings. We must broaden our scope of environmental impact to include the natural environment given to humans as well as the environment created by humans which begs for attention.

Francesco Venezia articulates this symbiotic relationship that might exist. The architect, "starting from an abstract control of, and at the same time in a sort of opposition to Nature, . . . should be able to create special harmony between his work and that of Nature and, in so doing, he should be able to make Nature freely work, on its highest level, to man's advantage."[120]

Thus the dialectical relationship between human/nature, urban form/ environment is removed. In addition to the natural world, we have created an artificial nature that has come to be our environment. The man-made environment, in a sense, must also be considered part of the natural state of things. This becomes another layer of environmental text which must be extracted and assessed.

1.3 PLANNING AND BUILDING REGULATIONS

Planning and building regulations form the third category of public architecture. Zoning is the common tool for planning control including land use and building form. The building code ensures functional, structural, and life-safety aspects of the building itself. They both are mechanisms to safeguard total development, both interior and exterior, for public health and safety. They are perhaps the most traditional means of achieving an orderly architecture of the city and a quality built environment. Therefore, we must examine these mechanisms.

Irvine

Irvine, California, is an excellent example of interwoven processes. We have already discussed the fact that Irvine requires a detailed architectural plan in the initial stages of the design evaluation process handled by The Irvine Company. Therefore, when the city begins its zoning compliance study leading to the issuing of a building permit, many items are already in place. However, the city must assure itself that a project fits into the long-range master plan; sometimes consultants assist with this evaluation. Also, the technical aspects of a project are checked. The Engineering Services Division of the Community Development Department reviews all building plans including the landscaping and grading. The Development Services Division looks at proposed development and participates in the processing of approved plans.

Requirements for new commercial/industrial and residential projects are quite similar. For both kinds of projects, information for a building plan check is sought:

- complete architectural and structural plans
- complete electrical, plumbing, and mechanical plans
- energy conservation standards
- soil report
- engineer's structural calculations

The Division of Current Planning checks:

- site plan with dimensions
- statistical inventory on site plan including:
  - square footage of site and of building footprint
  - percentage of site covered by building(s)
  - square footage in building(s) by use
  - square footage in parking area and landscaping
  - parking requirements
- details of fencing construction and materials, and of carports
- address of application (if no address is yet assigned)
- landscaping and irrigation plan

The division that reviews grading plans requires precise plans unless they were approved prior to building plans. Environmental Services asks that architects for projects in certain areas of the city submit a report showing how noise levels are to be mitigated. The Irvine Ranch Water District checks all projects served by the district before approval of plumbing plans.[121] To assure that no slips occur in the compliance process, the Community Development Department maintains a development case file on each project and a "Code Compliance Review" flowchart with written procedures for department personnel.[122]

Minneapolis

Minneapolis's *Zoning Code* allows a delay of up to a year between concept plan evaluation and approval and the preparation of final plans for apartment developments and their submission to the Department of Inspections. The zoning administrator keeps a file on each project from the time it enters the system to its eventual disposition, noting approval or disapproval and changes. The Department of Inspections is responsible for technical checking of plans submitted to it for approval. The zoning administrator will give the plans a final check to be sure that they are consistent with approved concept plans before issuing the necessary permits.

The planning staff reviews all site and building plans for clusterhome developments in its advisory capacity to the City Planning Commission. The staff check for zoning code and comprehensive plan compliance and coordinate reviews by other city departments. For example, the Zoning Office of the Building Inspection Department participates in zoning evaluations. This is a straightforward procedure with approval within 30 days if all ordinance requirements are met. The planning commission follows a similar process leading to approval of automobile-related usages (fast-food businesses, restaurants, etc.). Again, in these two cases, the role of the zoning administrator is the same in the final checking and issuing of a building permit.

All of the various districts—office-residence; community; central; downtown; commercial; and light, limited, and general manufacturing districts—and the Minnesota Technology Corridor have FAR and yard requirements. In certain districts—single; single- and two-family; single-, two-family, and townhouse; and general districts—the zoning code talks about building bulk limitations (rather than FARs and yard requirements). Parking requirements differ considerably in the various districts; only limited parking is permitted downtown. The planning department and other city agencies review all these details and report their findings to the City Planning Commission.

Baltimore

There are two additional steps (to those previously mentioned for other cities) in design evaluation by Baltimore's Design Advisory Panel (DAP): Step II, Preliminary Plans; and Step III, Final Plans. As might be expected, these two steps build consecutively and in more detail on the concept plan evaluation we have discussed previously. In Step II, we find a new emphasis on a landscape plan, with plant list, building elevations, section and floor plans, lighting and graphics, color samples of exterior materials, explanation of revised site plan (if required), explanation of building elevation and sections, fenestration and entrances, roof design, materials and colors, description of floor plans (size of rooms, hallways, kitchens, etc.), and lobby and building security measures. In Step III are final explanations of all Step I and Step II items with scale models, if desired.[123]

A very helpful pamphlet, "Development Guidebook: Requirements for Building in Baltimore City," clearly outlines the steps in obtaining a building permit. First, the Zoning Enforcement Section of the Neighborhood Progress Administration (NPA) checks that "proposed use is in compliance with existing zoning requirements." Then, the Special Referrals Section of the NPA looks to see if the project is in an area subject to special review (e.g., urban renewal, historic district, parking lot district, Critical Areas Zone, etc.). The third agency to inspect the plans is the Plan Examining Section of the NPA, which reviews them for "completeness of structural calculations, materials specifications, engineer's certificate, etc."[124] The NPA issues a receipt for the applicant's plans, sends copies to the appropriate agencies, and keeps a record of the progress of the plan evaluations.

If questions arise, it may be necessary for the applicant to meet with one or more of the agencies to which the plans have been referred in Step III. There may be queries from one of the many sections of the Department of Public Works that handle property location, grading, highway design, sediment and erosion control, water, or water supply, etc. Or the health and fire departments may have questions, too.

The fourth step is a review by the Site Plan Committee, a special inter-agency committee that provides a "one-stop" evaluation of the site plan. There are representatives from the departments of transit, traffic, public works, fire, NPA, and planning. The committee scrutinizes the more technical aspects of the plans such as pedestrian safety, fire lanes, traffic impact of the development, access for the handicapped, etc. The architect may ask for a preliminary review of the site plans prior to formal evaluation by the Site Plan Committee. In the fifth step, the Plan Examining Section notifies the applicant that the evaluation process has been properly completed, receives the necessary fees, and issues a building permit. During the construction, the NPA carries out various building inspections, and the Department of Public Works inspects for sediment and erosion control, utility connections, and footways and driveways.

A slightly different process occurs when a building permit is sought for a project in the Critical Areas Zone (within 1000 feet of the shoreline). State regulations apply, and the planning commission must review applications for building permits. In historical districts or for historical landmarks, special evaluation by the Commission for Historical and Architectural Preservation must determine the appropriateness of the project. The commission then issues a "notice to proceed." After all other regular requirements have been met, the NPA will issue a building permit in the usual way.

Urban renewal projects also necessitate special evaluations. First, the NPA makes a study of need for the project. A PAC, a representative neighborhood group for the affected area, has input into the process. The mayor and city council must approve the renewal plans, and the commissioner of the NPA makes final decisions on renewal standards. Changes in zoning will require approval by the city council as well. The applicant next moves to the DAP evaluation and proceeds through the zoning compliance review detailed above.

Small wonder that the city maintains offices to assist developers and their architects with general information and financing details. Charles Center, Inner Harbor Management, Market Center Development Corporation, and Baltimore Economic Development Corporation all maintain special offices for marketing, managerial, and planning assistance. The last entity has an "ombudsman service that cuts through red tape" for developers of joint ventures.[125] The Finance and Development Center of the NPA provides "a one-stop shopping service to developers, homeowners, and prospective house buyers who wish to purchase, renovate, or develop property in Baltimore City."[126] The center also aids in obtaining loans and moving the project through the building permit process.

Dallas

Returning again to a proposed project in the Near Eastside District, Dallas, let us assume that it has passed the design standards test and has accumulated enough points and has met "all other requirements of the construction codes and other applicable ordinances."[127] The director of planning then sends the application (and attached plans, etc.) on to the building official who issues a building permit. This process is supposed to be accomplished within 30 days. We must read between the lines to learn the rigor of meeting "all other requirements." If the project does not receive approval from the director of planning, the applicant may appeal that decision "by filing a written request with the department of planning and development within 10 days of the denial of the building permit."[128]

The site plan that has passed the Development Impact Review (as required in certain Dallas districts) is valid for two years. The building official must issue a building permit for the project in that site plan. However, "an approved site plan does not preclude the building official from refusing to issue a permit if he determines that plans and specifications do not comply with applicable laws and ordinances or that work does not conform to building code requirements."[129] Note that the planning staff as well as the Public Works, Building Inspection, and Transportation departments also review the site plan.

In historic districts, an added step in the evaluation process is the requirement for a Certificate of Appropriateness certifying that the proposed project meets district design criteria. Are the criteria for appropriateness a set of static rules, or are they allowed to change and grow in a dynamic process just as the architecture of the historic periods was ever-changing? Ordinance 18563 for the Swiss Avenue Historic District details exact specifications for buildings and landscaping and gives the director of planning authority to issue a Certificate of Appropriateness for limited routine maintenance or replacement and minor exterior alterations. All other projects require review by the design committee and the planning commission according to the specified standards prior to the issuance of a Certificate of Appropriateness. The next step in both cases (if all other requirements have been met) is issuance of a building permit. Appeals go to the city council for resolution.

Indianapolis

As in Dallas, Certificates of Appropriateness are a part of the review process in Indianapolis's historic areas. Actually, in the Wholesale District Historic Area, only demolition work requires a Certificate of Appropriateness or a Certificate of Authorization from the Indianapolis Historic Preservation Commission. All other types of construction or renovation do not require the certificate. Nor does any work that is being done on a project receiving federal monies and subject to review by the Advisory Council on Historic Preservation, a federal agency, have to undergo additional Indianapolis scrutiny.

Kansas City

Continuing our previous discussion of the Redevelopment Authority in Kansas City and its design evaluation, we find an example of overlap of procedures. Recall that the first stage of evaluation, Schematic Design, required but a description of technical details of the project. The second phase, Design Development, is to "secure agreement on and approval of final design prior to extensive and detailed work on the preliminary working drawings." Now, the third and last phase is Final Working Drawings and Specifications with approval sought for "the contract documents and the complete proposal."[130]

   The City Plan Commission (with help of the planning staff) generally is responsible for the technical evaluation leading to issuance of a building permit—if successful. The planning staff often meets several times with a developer and architect in an effort to help them prepare for the formal evaluation. In most parts of Kansas City, it is possible for persons wishing to make additions to existing or related buildings or to construct a new one- or two-family dwelling to submit their own plans for the project, if they wish, as long as they can comply with the regulations. Only new multifamily and commercial buildings require the services of an architect or engineer licensed in Missouri, and

   the plans should show pertinent architectural, structural, plumbing, mechanical, fire protection, elevator and foundation details in accordance with applicable zoning ordinances and city building codes.[131]

The City Plan Commission also sits as the Board of Zoning Adjustment.[132] The County Circuit Court hears appeals from decisions of the Board of Zoning Adjustment.[133]

San Francisco

Our first discussion of San Francisco's public architecture leaned heavily on provisions of the second Proposition M. Dealing with all those details is just the beginning of running the gamut of requirements for office buildings. The architect already has applied for Project Authorization to attempt to meet Proposition M requirements and initiate the building permit process. The City Planning Commission acts on project authorizations and building permit applications. The architect may appeal a negative response "to the Board of Permit Appeals . . . within ten days of Commission action."[134]

Meanwhile, the developers of other projects have their own problems to solve. For all developers and their architects, San Francisco's emphasis on informal sessions to iron out difficulties is a blessing in the midst of the maze. Buildings of less than 15,000 gsf are reviewed by the planning staff and approved administratively if there are no hitches: zoning changes, conditional uses, etc. It is the larger projects, however, that are of natural concern because of their potential for more noticeable adverse effects.

Architects are in a demanding position. Here the main keys to approval are conformance with the Master Plan and any other pertinent plan (e.g., special or preservation district plans) as well as with all building code details. Of course, there may be complications: the need for conditional uses, TDR, unsuitable environmental impact, etc. Note that public hearings are a part of the process, too. There will be extensive planning staff evaluation of all project details and review by other city agencies.

Finally, let us consider briefly the permit process for preservation of buildings and districts of architectural, historic, and aesthetic importance in the C-3 districts, downtown San Francisco. The city bases its procedures on a firm base of carefully written descriptions and standards of preservation. Complicating things is the possibility of making alterations that would enable the lot on which a building is sited to be declared eligible for Compatible Rehabilitation designation and, hence, eligible as a preservation lot for TDR.[135]

The planning director (with the aid of the planning staff) makes recommendations to the planning commission concerning approval or disapproval of alterations and compatible rehabilitations. Disapproval by the planning commission means a recommendation to the Central Permit Bureau that a permit be denied. If the director of planning has recommended approval to the planning commission and they disagree, they must give their reasons for failure to support the recommendation. The planning commission's refusal to grant a compatible rehabilitation status is a "final administrative decision."[136] Section 1111.6 of *Zoning Ordinance* 414-85, Article II, gives clear and specific "standards and requirements for review of applications for alterations."

San Diego

Getting approval for a project gets complicated in a city like San Diego with its highly organized layer-on-layer of urban design and zoning and building code regulations. For example, in the *Centre City Overlay Zone User's Guide,* one reads through the "Application Review Process" on page 2 and the "Centre City Advisory Committee" description on page 3 and comes away with an understanding of the permit process in this particular area of San Diego. Yet on page 1 is additional information:

> As the name implies, the Centre City Overlay Zone is a set of standards that works with, and is in addition to, the underlying zoning. So the requirements contained therein are simply "overlayed" on top of existing zoning regulations. If there is a conflict between them, the requirements of the underlying zone will take precedence.
>
> The underlying zone also determines the permitted use of the site. Conditional Use Permits are required for discrete parking facilities, including surface parking lots. Applications for Conditional Use Permits are reviewed by the Zoning Administrator.[137]

The city's permit process is clear and straightforward as outlined in the *User's Guide,* but there are several important issues. Those projects which conform to Overlay Zone regulation may receive approval. "May" is the word used in the *User's Guide* (p. 2). However, those applications and plans that do not meet overlay zone regulations may receive approval if the project meets the following conditions:

1. Fulfills an individual and/or community need without negatively affecting the community or General Plan, and
2. Is not detrimental to other properties in the area or to people living or working in the area, and
3. Meets the purpose and intent of the Overlay Zone.[138]

The Centre City Advisory Committee (appointed by the mayor and city council) hears appeals from the planning director's denial.

The *User's Guide* warns: "It is important that all of the necessary information be provided or delays in the processing of your application may occur."

Of course, there is the special "Centre City Overlay Zone Application Form," but in addition the architect must submit:

1. Information on the purpose of the building with proposed uses of each level specified.
2. "Two (2) copies of fully dimensioned plans and specifications (plot plan)" including lot area, lot coverage, floor area, FAR, etc.
3. "Two (2) copies of fully dimensioned plans . . . that illustrate conformance to each requirement of the Overlay Zone. . . ."[139]

The standards to be met:

1. "Two (2) copies of fully dimensioned plans and specifications for any accessory buildings, . . . fences/walls, . . . street furniture," etc.
2. "Any other information deemed necessary by the Planning Director to judge compliance with the Overlay Zone regulations."
3. Fees.[140]

What does not appear in the process as outlined in the *User's Guide* is the basic San Diego code requirements that also must be met.

Now then, suppose the architect's project is in Southeast San Diego Planned District. The ordinance covering regulations here is 0-16921 (new series) approved August 3, 1987.

> Application, including fee/deposit schedule, notification and appeal procedures for a Southeast San Diego Development Permit shall be consistent with the Planned Residential Development Permit (Section 101.0900) for residential projects, with the Planned Commercial Development Permit (Section 101.0910) for commercial projects and with the Planned Industrial Development Permit (Section 101.0920) for industrial projects.[141]

The basic city standards are upfront this time: If the project conforms to "all City regulations, policies, guidelines, design standards and density, the Planning Director shall grant a Southeast San Diego Development Permit within 90 days." But wait! There is more: Providing

1. Environmental review standards are met.
2. The use and project design meet Southeast San Diego standards and do not adversely affect neighboring plans, "the General Plan or other applicable plans adopted by City Council."
3. The proposed development is "compatible with existing and planned land use on adjoining properties, [is not] a disruptive element, [and is in] architectural harmony."

4. "The proposed use, because of conditions that have been applied to it, will not be detrimental to the health, safety and general welfare of persons residing or working in the area, and will not adversely affect other property in the vicinity."
5. "The proposed use will comply with the relevant regulations in the Code."[142]

Add to this the discretionary permit design review by the Southeast Economic Development Corporation's Board of the Southeast San Diego Community Planning Committee and the "additional focused development criteria . . . established per neighborhood requirements."[143] Certainly, the architect will check the list of permitted uses in the Southeast San Diego District. Does the developer plan a project that is permitted, not permitted? Or is it subject to limitations or a special permit? It makes a difference, naturally, whether this project is planned for a residential, commercial, or industrial zone.

Seattle

Stringent zoning ordinances on top of the already described urban design evaluation make development a process not to be undertaken lightly in Seattle. The Long Range Planning Commission has recently revised the Comprehensive Plan and prepared new zoning regulations. Building permits are issued by the director of the Department of Construction and Land Use. In the case of the Harvard-Belmont Landmark District, issuance of a Certificate of Approval by the Seattle Landmarks Preservation Board comes after a project has met district standards. A board hearing is part of the proceedings, too. The Certificate of Approval is needed for significant changes to buildings and other structures.

It would appear that the director may process other aspects of a building permit application as the effort to obtain a Certificate of Approval continues. In Section 8 of Ordinance 109388 we find the statement:

> The Director shall continue to process the application, but shall not issue any permit until a Certificate of Approval has been issued . . . or the time for filing the notice of denial of a Certificate of Approval with the Director has expired.[144]

Appeals of a denial of a Certificate of Approval are heard by the hearing examiner.

A project may require two permits, a Master Use Permit covering zoning issues and a Building Permit indicating compliance with construction requirements and the building code. There are five types of zoning decisions made by the Department of Construction and Land Use. As might be expected, the first is administerial; that is, routine matters are handled by the staff. Type two decisions involve discretion; these are the responsibility of the director. Again, the hearing examiner receives appeals to the director's decisions. Types three to five entail environmental review and quasi-judicial and legislative decisions by city council, for example, rezonings or new zoning, respectively.

Vail

In Vail, the Design Review Board (DRB) handles the preliminary/final review of a project. Vail administers design evaluation on a very detailed basis in this preliminary/final review phase. The zoning administrator may rule that some of the following information is not necessary:

1. Topographic survey indicating present site conditions
2. Preliminary title report
3. Detailed drainage plan
4. Detailed site plan
5. Verification of utilities availability
6. Landscape plan
7. Preliminary architectural plans including labeled floor plans, elevations, exterior surfacing, materials including samples; the architect shows how building will look through sketches, scale models, or photographic overlays
8. Scale drawings of signage
9. Plan for erosion control and revegetation

The staff of the Community Development Department (CDD) again evaluates the project. Is it in "compliance with applicable provisions of the zoning code subdivision regulations, 18.54.040C.1 [items listed above]?" If the DRB finds that the project does "comply with the objectives and design guidelines of this chapter," they approve the design of the project, sometimes conditionally.[145] The DRB sends its recommendation to the city council, who must act, approving or disapproving it. Meetings of the DRB and the city council are open to the public.

Zoning Regulations

Zoning regulations have been in effect in the United States since 1916 and have contributed to the livability of many of its cities. As the design evaluation process grows ever more complex and the issues become more interwoven, the zoning requirements, too, become fragmented and their implementation is determined and overseen by several different agencies. In some cities the zoning regulations have become part of the criteria for architectural concept. The zoning requirements differ from city to city and in themselves can determine a great deal about its texture. However, the implementation of these objective guidelines can in some cases contribute to the codification and uniformity of cities across the country instead of adding to their dynamic individual character.

Architects are, of course, the custodians of health, safety, and welfare; and there is no question about the necessity of the regulations and guidelines that exist. As we have seen through our discussion here, however, it is not always easy to extract these issues from the layers of guidelines that are in operation.

1.4 THE COMMON GROUND

Obviously, there are areas of overlap among the three categories, because in general these evaluation guidelines have as a goal the *appropriateness* and *compatibility* of a development project within a contextual base, the existing architectural and urban fabric—a goal that may itself need some critical rethinking.

The 12 cities studied here all have processes in place; they vary, however, in their incorporation of the three categories as well as their strategy for evaluation implementation. Some cities use all three categories, some only two of the three; some have extensive, lengthy means of execution, while others maintain a process of relatively few steps. Some have exacting guidelines and publications to illustrate and interpret what is expected, and others have very little published documentation at the disposal of the architect. These points have been clearly—granted at times, tediously—presented in this chapter. The fundamental consideration that the evaluation apparatus fails to confront is the true nature of the public architecture it aims to achieve.

The institutionalization of the process has led these cities to assemble similar blueprints for design. Initial models and premises that are virtually the same or moving toward each other lead to specifications and guidelines for a generic architecture of the city. In these processes, as we will see later in this book, the institution has taken over the substantive elements of design. While the translation of these criteria into the design is the prerogative of architects, they must be ready to fit their projects and their ideas into the framework of pertinent regulations.

There is a fine line between the compatibility the city seeks and the architect's design concept which is based on both insight and the client's (developer's) need. This process has not been altogether successful in generating an architecture of substance. Often design solutions fashioned under these procedures are simply the physical evidence of the process void of the substantive element that is so needed. Bernard Tschumi attempts to bridge the gap between process and substance in "La Case Vide"—La Villette plan in Paris. "A moment in the process of conception, the ephemeral and temporary material-ization of concept. . . . On one hand, the constructions on the site are real, material; on the other, they are abstract notations in a process."[146]

The notions of compatibility and compliance pop up constantly through-out the reading of the ordinances, plans, and guidelines. Good design judged through the validation of the new by existing context and a reliance on style rather than substance as a mediation between present and proposed form permeate the design guideline documentation. It follows the thinking of urban design proposals by Leon Krier and Christopher Alexander. Alexander sees the building as an increment of the larger context. It must not only establish its own center but reinforce those centers already existing and contribute to a future center that is not yet a reality.[147] Thus the new structure must complete, validate, and anticipate the text. The guidelines for San Francisco listed earlier are full of comparable requirements for built form and its relationship to an existing context.

Establishing parameters within which to create built form takes precedence over establishing a system of design innovation and of testing the limits of the tools that are available to the architect. The result of such a process of design through compliance and regulation "is the one which involves the right choice of means to given ends . . . specified in functional terms. . . . To each of these functions is assigned a mechanism for its fulfillment . . . [causing] the city itself to be divided up into ends and means."[148]

The architectural concept is often judged by standards that are applied as blanket requirements rather than reference guidelines, leaving little room for the architect to practice his or her craft. In some cases, as in Baltimore, the architect is even given advice on aesthetics. Environmental impact concerns are treated in a piecemeal fashion in most cities and need to be further enhanced in their current direction. However, the cities also need to attempt to deal with the naturalness of "man's inhabited and constructed realm . . . at once the *natural* and the *artificial* homeland of man."[149]

> Perhaps a broader definition of context is required as well. The new context then is not just the physical setting or the methods and styles of contemporary building, or relevant historical and metaphorical references; it is also in the broadest sense an understanding of how the world around one works and the melding of this into physical patterns of order which both function and uplift.[150]

Attempts to institutionalize the design evaluation process for public architecture have been made throughout the last decade. In some cases this has been realized—San Francisco, for example. The results of the widespread use of the design guideline process are, however, obviously in question here and in the critical investigations going on in urban architecture. Once put into motion, these regulations, guidelines, rules, and suggestions tend to remain in place past their shelf life, perpetuating a process for the production of static architecture.[151]

What does the architecture of the city tell us about the success of the design evaluation processes at work across the United States? Can design evaluation help the city obtain the elusive factor, ambience, that makes a city unique? Maintaining ambience seems to make the city more attractive to development, threatening the very character that brought development in the first place. However, this "ambience" is often falsely attempted or achieved through the fostering of artificial nostalgia, resulting in empty replicas of an irrelevant past. And frequently the design guidelines laid out in the evaluation process "are used to rectify . . . what is essentially an incoherent or poorly articulated physical context."[152]

As with all institutions, a whole apparatus is needed to perpetuate the system, verifying, codifying, regulating, but rarely updating the process. This bureaucratic infrastructure is the topic of the next chapter.

REFERENCE NOTES

1. Jacquelin Robertson, "The Current Crisis of Disorder," in *The Public Face of Architecture,* ed. Nathan Glazer and Mark Lilla (New York: Free Press, 1987), 484.
2. The Irvine Company, "Westpark Design Guidelines," April 25, 1985 (revised February 28, 1986), 1.
3. City of Portland (OR), "Terwilliger Parkway Design Guidelines," 1983, 1.
4. City of Portland, Design Commission, "Design Review Application and Submission Requirements," August 1984, 1.
5. Ibid., 2.
6. Quality Urban Environment Study Team (QUEST), "Minneapolis Saint Paul [MN]," Urban Planning and Design Committee/American Institute of Architects, May 14-17, 1981, 5-6.
7. City of Minneapolis, *Zoning Code,* 534.450.(1), Supp. No. 1, June 1976, 3778.1.
8. Sydney Brower, "Baltimore's Design Review and Management System," *HUD Challenge* (January 1977):17.
9. City of Baltimore (MD), "Design Advisory Panel Guidelines" (revised), October 1983, 1.
10. Douglas Waskom, Chief Planner, Development Review, Department of Planning and Development, City of Dallas (TX), letter to the author, May 26, 1986, 2.
11. City of Dallas, Department of Planning, "Development Impact Review," Paper No. 1978T/22T, n.d., 1.

12. City of Dallas, Department of Planning, "Amending Ordinance 18312" (draft), Section 1, December 13, 1985, 2.
13. Ibid.
14. Marion County and Indianapolis (IN), *City County General Ordinance No. 13,* "Regional Center Zoning Ordinance," amending Marion County Council Ordinance No. 8-1957, Section 2, January 31, 1983, 2.
15. Ibid.
16. Indianapolis Historic Preservation Commission, "Lockerbie Square Plan Design Standards," January 1987, D1.
17. *Ordinances of the City of Lincoln [NE],* Chapter 14.90.015,532.13-14.
18. Ibid., .020 and .025, 532.14.
19. Ibid., .025 (c) and (d), 532.15.
20. Ibid., (e).
21. City of Kansas City (MO), "River City Rehab: Recognizing Your Architectural Assets," 1980, Preface.
22. City of Kansas City, City Development Department, "The Plaza Urban Design and Development Plan," January 1988, 114-115.
23. City of Kansas City, "Board of Trade Urban Renewal Plan," September 24, 1986, Exhibit J., 1.
24. Ibid., 2.
25. Richard L. Williams, "How to Get on Top as a City: Attract Do-gooders Who Do," *Smithsonian* (March 1979):105.
26. Hamid Shirvani, *Urban Design Review* (Chicago: Planner's Press, 1981).
27. Frank Viviano and Sharon Silvä, "Make No Little Plans," *TWA Ambassador* (January 1986):56.
28. Gary Delsohn, "Putting a Cap on Boxy High-Rises," *The Denver Post* (June 1, 1986): G1.
29. Dean L. Macris, "Memorandum to City Planning Commission," February 2, 1987, in "Rules for the 1986-87 Approval Period of the Office Development Limitation Program (Annual Limit)," as adopted by the City (of San Francisco CA) Planning Commission, Exhibit A, February 5, 1987, 1.
30. City of San Francisco, *Zoning Ordinances,* 414.85, Article I, Section 321 (b).1, October 17, 1985, 78.
31. Dean L. Macris, "Memorandum to City Planning Commission," 5.
32. Ibid., 7-8.
33. Ibid., 10.
34. City of San Diego (CA), Department of Planning, *What Is City Planning in San Diego?* c. 1985, 6.
35. Ibid., 5.
36. Ibid., 19.
37. Ibid., 19-20.
38. Ibid., 20.
39. Roger Showley, " 'Paradise' Policies 10 Years Later," *The San Diego Union* (September 16, 1984): F1.
40. City of San Diego, Centre City Development Corporation, *Urban Design Program Centre City San Diego,* October 25, 1983, 64.

41. City of San Diego, Department of Planning, "Urban Design Program Update," Information Report No. 87-644, December 4, 1987, 1.
42. City of Seattle (WA), Ordinance 109388.6, August 26, 1980, 11.
43. Ibid., 11-12.
44. Ibid., 12.
45. Thomas A. Braun, Senior Planner, Town of Vail (CO), letter to the author, April 22, 1986, 1.
46. Ibid., 2.
47. Thomas A. Braun and Jeffrey Winston, "The Vail Village Urban Design Guide Plan: A Framework for Guiding Development," *UD Review* 9, No. 4 (Fall 1986): 13.
48. Town of Vail, *Zoning Title,* 18.54.040.B.2, November 5, 1983, 451.
49. Ibid., 040.B.1, 450.
50. Joseph Rykwert, "The Street: The Use of Its History," in *On Streets,* ed. Stanford Anderson (Cambridge, MA: MIT Press, 1986), 15.
51. Robert Gutman, "Educating Architects: Pedagogy and the Pendulum," in *The Public Face of Architecture,* 456-7.
52. Ibid., 455-456.
53. Hamid Shirvani, "Architecture Versus Franchised Design," *Urban Design and Preservation Quarterly* 11, No. 2/3 (1988): 5.
54. Pierluigi Nicolin, "Architecture Between Representation and Projects," in *Beyond the City, the Metropolis,* ed. Georges Teyssot (Milan: Electra, 1988), 277.
55. Hamid Shirvani, "City as Artifact," *Urban Design International* 8, No. 1 (1988).
56. Hamid Shirvani, *The Urban Design Process* (New York: Van Nostrand Reinhold, 1985), 69-70.
57. Ibid., 72.
58. Town of Vail, *Zoning Title* 18.02.020.B, 1973, 301-302.
59. Ibid., 18.54.010, November 15, 1983, 7.
60. Ibid., .040.C, 452, 454.
61. Ibid., .050.D, 454g.
62. Ibid., .051.E, December 23, 1986, 454j-455.
63. Town of Vail, "Vail Village Design Considerations," June 11, 1980, 10.
64. Ibid., draft of revision, 1986, 24.
65. Town of Vail, "Vail Land Use Plan," November 18, 1986, 6-7.
66. Ibid., 31.
67. City of San Diego, Department of Planning, "Resource Protection Overlay Zone Informational Booklet," September 1987, 13.
68. City of San Diego, Department of Planning, *Mid-City Community Plan,* 1984 (as amended through May 27, 1986), 7.
69. Ibid., 15.
70. Ibid., 40.
71. Ibid., 158.
72. Ibid., 161.
73. Ibid., 164.
74. Ibid., 118.

75. City of San Diego, Department of Planning, "Mid-City Community Plan Amendment" (draft), "Normal Heights" (supplement), October 2, 1987, 10.
76. Ibid., "Kensington" (supplement), 24; "Talmadge" (supplement), 36.
77. City of Portland, Bureau of Planning, *Downtown Design Guidelines,* 1983, 54.
78. City of Portland, Bureau of Planning, *Downtown Plan Handbook,* 1981, 42.
79. Ibid., 45.
80. City of Portland, "Steps in the Historical Landmarks Commission Review Procedure," January 26, 1984, 2.
81. City of Portland, *Zoning Code,* Title 33.215.120.B.3, "Application Requirements," July 18, 1985, 20.
82. City of Portland, Bureau of Planning, *Recommended Central City Plan,* January 1988, 7.
83. City of Portland, *Amendments to Recommended Central City Plan,* Section 33.702.080, March 1988, 41.
84. City of Seattle, *Policies and Procedures [of the Design Commission],* n.d., 11.
85. Ibid.
86. Ibid., 12.
87. City of Seattle, *Zoning Code,* Chapter 23.56.02, "Overlay Districts, Purpose," n.d., 1.
88. State of Washington, *Washington Administrative Code,* Chapter 197-11, *Washington State Environmental Policy Act (SEPA) Rules* (Olympia: Department of Ecology, 1984), Foreword.
89. City of Seattle, City Council Staff, "Seattle 2000 Action Inventory: An Inventory of City Actions Related to the Seattle 2000 Goals, 1973-1984," Final Working Draft, May 1985, V-36-37.
90. William D. Schaefer, letter to the citizens of Baltimore, in "Street Tree Planting Standards," Baltimore City Department of Parks and Recreation, 1985, Foreword.
91. City of Baltimore, Neighborhood Progress Administration, *Baltimore City Neighborhoods, 1984-87,* n.d., 49.
92. Ibid., quote from Peter Fender, Tindeco resident, 52.
93. City of Baltimore, Baltimore City Department of Housing and Community Development, "Inner Harbor Project I Renewal Plan," originally approved June 15, 1967, with amendments through May 8, 1985, 3-4.
94. City of Baltimore, "Baltimore City Neighborhoods," 10.
95. City of Baltimore, Baltimore City Department of Planning, "Baltimore's Development Program, 1988-1993," 1987, 116.
96. Ibid., 156.
97. Ibid., 159.
98. Vincent Ponte and Warren Travers, letter of transmittal preceding "A Report on Parks, Boulevards and Special Streets," in *Dallas Downtown Plan 1986,* September 15, 1986.
99. City of Dallas, Department of Urban Planning, "Procedures for Filling in a Flood Plain Under the Flood Plain Management Guidelines," October 1977, 3.

100. Ibid., 3–4.

101. City of Dallas, "Ordinance 17216, "Escarpment Zone Regulations," November 1981, 1–2.

102. City of Dallas, Department of Planning and Development, "Dallas CBD Pedestrian Facilities, Summary Report," January 1982, 5.

103. City of Lincoln, "Report from the Mayor's Ad Hoc Committee on Project Design," August 5, 1986, 5.

104. Ibid., 5–7.

105. Ibid., attachment of Interdepartment Communication, Urban Design Committee to Mayor Luedtke, "Statement of urban design concerns regarding downtown project," August 5, 1986, 5.

106. City of Indianapolis, "Draft for Sky Exposure Plane Standard," attachment, "Existing Sky Exposure Plane Standards," April 5, 1988, 16–17 (original paging, 29–30).

107. City of Indianapolis, "Draft for Sky Exposure Plane Standard," 2.

108. Joann Green, Kevin Parsons, et al., "Old Plans, New Projects: Indianapolis Finds Itself," *Landscape Architecture* 73, No. 4 (July 1983):83.

109. City of Kansas City, City Development Department, *Kansas City Urban Design Guidebook,* 1978, 5.

110. Ibid., 107.

111. City of Kansas City, Redevelopment Authority, "Downtown Streetscape Manual," May 6, 1985 (and updated), 2.

112. Judy Hansen, memorandum to team members, "A City Plan for Urban Design and Development Policy" (proposed), September 23, 1987, 26.

113. Ibid., 41.

114. City of Kansas City, Planning Division, "A City Plan for Urban Design and Development Policy," c1987, 1.

115. City of Minneapolis, City Planning Department, *State of the City 1983,* January 1984, 57.

116. Ibid., 77–84.

117. City of Minneapolis, City Planning Department, *Metro 2000 Plan,* January 1988, 5.

118. City of Minneapolis, City Planning Department, *Minneapolis Metro Center Planning Principles,* August 1978, C-28.

119. City of Minneapolis, City Planning Department, *Minneapolis Metro Center Plan 1990,* July 1978, D-37.

120. Francesco Venezia, "Architecture/Nature," *Utopica* 2 (1988):8.

121. City of Irvine, "Submittal Checklists for 'Commercial/Industrial Plan Check (New Buildings)' [and for] 'Residential Plan Check (New Homes),'" PHB 222-04/CDD(5) and PHB 222-05/CDD(5) (revised February 1988), 2.

122. City of Irvine, "Code Compliance Review Process," June 7, 1984.

123. City of Baltimore, "Design Advisory Panel Guidelines," 1.

124. City of Baltimore, "Development Guidebook: Requirements for Building in Baltimore City," 3rd ed., revised April 1985, 4.

125. Ibid., 16.

126. Ibid., 18.
127. City of Dallas, Department of Planning, "Amending Ordinance 18312" (draft), 9.
128. Ibid.
129. City of Dallas, Department of Planning, "Development Impact Review," 2.
130. Kansas City Missouri Redevelopment Authority, "Board of Trade Urban Renewal Plan," 2-3.
131. City of Kansas City, Public Information Office, "How to Obtain a Building Permit," April 1987, 4.
132. *Charter of Kansas City,* Section 403, adopted 1925, as amended September 1985, 649.
133. City of Kansas City, *Zoning Ordinances,* 55516.39.320, January 9, 1984 (revised January 1987), 140.
134. Dean L. Macris, "Memorandum," 14.
135. City of San Francisco, *Zoning Ordinances,* 414-85.II.1111, October 17, 1985, 90.
136. Ibid., 1111.5, 91.
137. City of San Diego, *Centre City Overlay Zone User's Guide,* March 2, 1987, 1.
138. Ibid., 2.
139. Ibid., 13.
140. Ibid., 24.
141. City of San Diego, "Southeast San Diego Planned District," Ordinance 0-16921 (new series), Section 101.1702.B.2, August 3, 1987, 3.
142. Ibid., B.3, 3.
143. Ibid., E, 4.
144. City of Seattle, *Zoning Ordinances,* 109388.8, 12.
145. Town of Vail, *Zoning Title,* 18.54.040.C.2, 454b.
146. Bernard Tschumi, "La Case Vide," in Jacques Derrida, "Point de Folie—Maintenant L'Architecture: Bernard Tschumi: La Case Vide—La Villette, 1985," *AA Files* 12 (Summer 1986):66.
147. Christopher Alexander et al., *A New Theory of Urban Design* (New York: Oxford University Press, 1987).
148. Roger Scruton, "Public Space and the Classical Vernacular," in *The Public Face of Architecture,* 21.
149. Aldo Rossi, *The Architecture of the City* revised for the American edition by Aldo Rossi and Peter Eisenman (Cambridge, MA: MIT Press, 1982), 27.
150. Robertson, "The Current Crisis of Disorder," 487-488.
151. Hamid Shirvani, "Architecture Versus Franchised Design," 4.
152. Ibid.

Chapter 2

BUREAUCRATIC PROCESSES

Having presented public design evaluation categories in Chapter 1, in this chapter we focus on the models and administrative approaches used in public evaluation of the architecture of the city. It is certainly obvious that the present state of public evaluation in each of the cities is a result of a particular set of circumstances that have existed in that city over a period of years. However, by close examination of the 12 cities studied here, we can find a great deal of similarity in the bureaucratic nature of their procedures despite their individual urban and architectural history.

2.1 THE MODELS

In general, there are four basic approaches to public design evaluation: (1) discretionary, (2) flexible, (3) design option, and (4) self-administering.[1] These four divisions are identified in general terms; it is important to note that in some cases, a city's method of evaluation implementation is quite complicated and cannot be linked with any one of the four models. The opposite is also true, as there are cities that have an ad hoc or a mixed-bag approach that might be described as no formal approach at all.

When the standards and criteria for evaluation are left in the hands of a review body, we refer to that as a discretionary approach to design evaluation. This can be the deliberate approach of a city in that standards are generally stated or a high level of confidence in the evaluation body exists; or perhaps there are political reasons. It can also be a result of a city's lack of fixed or established standards for the evaluation of development projects. The review body makes a determination on the suitability of design for each project individually, considering the nature and merits of the project. In this case, the review body, the members of the design evaluation team, have (or have assumed) full discretion in determining standards and criteria for evaluation of a project.

The determination of suitability can be a highly subjective process. Depending on the nature of the evaluation board, their professional status, background, and political character, the outcome of the evaluation process may vary greatly from one discretionary body to another and from one project to another, even when evaluated by the same team. If a city has a flexible approach to design evaluation, there is some sort of framework and a general or overall design policy. There may be city zoning ordinances, as well as other types of development ordinances or architectural guidelines which impose design standards and criteria. These guidelines provide a general architectural design framework and not specific architecture or design prescriptions. This approach is certainly more desirable from the perspective of architectural creativity, innovation, and independent architectural thinking. Under this approach, the evaluation body has to work within established parameters, but they can act with some discretion in evaluating individual projects.

The third administrative approach to design evaluation is that of design option. Here the city has determined a sizable share of the design standards and criteria through city zoning ordinances or other self-explanatory development guidelines and controls. A developer and his or her design team read and apply these guidelines, controls, standards, and criteria to development projects; the evaluation body has the responsibility of checking to be sure the project "fits" the standards. Within this approach, the guidelines can be too rigid and restrictive from an architectural perspective; therefore, the products of this approach also can be monotonous and, frankly, dull.

Often, there are guidelines that are still left in the hands of the design evaluation body, but not much discretion is possible in exercising their responsibilities. Or, to put it in another way, in the design option approach there are established guidelines and criteria; but some are flexible options, and the architect for an individual project may select from among these options depending on the nature of the project. He or she may or may not choose an "appropriate" option. Evaluation then focuses on the compatibility of the selected options. While allowing flexibility within the design options, the evaluation of these options is still based on the traditional and subjective notions of appropriateness and fit.

Finally, there is the self-administering approach, implying that there is no need for a formal design evaluation process. All the established design criteria and guidelines are clearly defined, written, and/or illustrated. The architects and other members of the design team obtain these guidelines and apply them to the specific project that they are proposing. In this approach, of course, the architect has the right to meet with the planning and design officials in the city or community to ask for advice and explanations; hopefully, the city encourages this. There could be a number of informal design evaluation procedures but not one that is formally established. The self-administering procedure is even further limiting and restrictive than the design option approach and suggests a measure of superficiality in its methods. While some practitioners work well within these parameters, which seem to help focus their design energy, others may get bogged down following the recipe for design and lose sight of the innovative facets of the process. Still others are simply unable to work creatively within such restrictions.

If the reader concludes that these administrative approaches to design evaluation differ mainly in degree of rigidity, formality, and red tape, that may be a somewhat valid thought at this point. Let us see whether this conclusion is still in order when we finish analyzing the cities' administrative approaches.

2.2 CASE STUDIES

Baltimore

Baltimore's "Inner Harbor Project I Renewal Plan" quite clearly begins with a self-administering criterion.

> In order to achieve the objectives of the Renewal Plan, the uses, as defined in sub-sections 3.2., and B.3., below, are the only uses permitted on property to be acquired in the Project.[2]

Yet, on page 21 we find a design option item: "Maximum Permitted Height [commercial residential]: Elevation 190 feet, except for such vertical circulation elements and mechanical equipment as may be approved by the Department [under certain restrictions]."[3] Both the "Inner Harbor Project I Renewal Plan" and the "Urban Renewal Plan, Washington Hill-Chapel" (revised through 1985) are replete with general directives with very specific provisions that must be followed—all listed with the verb "shall".

Under the Inner Harbor "Aesthetic Controls and Reviews," we find very straightforward dicta: "Each developer will submit for all development . . . detailed preliminary plans and outline specifications . . . in sufficient detail to show site planning, architectural design and layout . . . [etc.]"[4] However, note the following, which indicates that the agency expects some of its decisions to be discretionary.

> Developers will be required to agree that, in the event of any question regarding the meaning of these standards or other provisions of this Plan, the interpretation placed thereon by the Agency shall be final and binding, provided that any such interpretation shall not be unreasonable or arbitrary.[5]

A quick review of the "Development Guide Book: Requirements for Building in Baltimore City" (April 1985) would convince an architect that most of the evaluation of his or her project will be self-administering. For example, in addition to all the detail we already mentioned, any planned construction that intrudes onto a public sidewalk or street requires a minor privilege granted by the Board of Estimates, or a franchise by ordinance of the city council for major intrusions.

However, as we shall discover in many of the cities, the guidelines for the Design Advisory Panel (DAP) indicate the discretionary nature of their evaluation.

> It is not the responsibility of the Panel to interfere with the normal relationship between the developer and his architect; nor is it the responsibility of the Panel to perform architectural services for the developer. While the Panel is interested in architectural treatment and may make suggestions for improvements, it is the architect's responsibility to make the final decisions regarding the design.[6]

Do not conclude that these suggestion can be ignored.

> Written comments made by the DAP shall be forwarded by certified mail to the developer within seven days of the presentations. These comments are to be addressed by the architect at the following presentation.[7]

Baltimore's "Historic Preservation Guidelines" are typical of those in many other cities.

> In accordance with its authority (Ordinance #939), the Commission for Historical and Architectural Preservation (CHAP) has adopted architectural guidelines to assist the property owner in formulating preservation plans. These advisory guidelines also serve to assist the Commission in determining the appropriateness of such plans. CHAP realizes that it must also consider economic hardship and particular structural factors.[8]

A little later in Section C we find:

> Paint colors must be submitted to CHAP for approval. Paint permits are issued upon receipt of paint samples. . . . Repainting should be done with color appropriate to the period of the building and neighborhood. Incompatible color contrast should be avoided. Upon request the CHAP office will assist in researching appropriate colors for the historic structure or district.

Also note:

> CHAP must approve the following: "any excavation, construction or erection of any building, fence, wall, or other structure of any kind; or for any removal of any external architectural feature, or for any reconstruction, alteration, change to exterior color by painting or other means, or for any demolition of any structure."[9]

Dallas

Dallas has realized the necessity for some discretion in the administering of its codes and ordinances. For example, a brochure, "Landmark Preservation Incentives for the City of Dallas Central Business District," says:

> While maintaining essential safety and welfare provisions, the City of Dallas can exercise some flexibility in the application of its construction and use codes where landmark structures are concerned. The City Plan Commissions's Landmark Committee monitors the code's impact on landmark renovation projects and periodically reports back to the City Council with recommendations for adjustments to the code and code enforcement procedures.[10]

The title of another Dallas publication, "Development Standards [for Oak Lawn Special Purpose District]," reveals the nature of the proposals submitted by Amphion Environmental, Inc., to the City of Dallas and Maple Avenue Economic Development Corporation, September 1985. Consider the following items:

1. "Access for parking lots must be from public alleys or adjacent side streets" (p. 5).
2. "An owner shall provide screening for the service side of a nonresidential building if the service side is exposed to and closer than 50 feet to the special retail street" (p. 11).

The consultants make many other suggestions for the development of this special purpose district which are added to the "shalls" and "musts" of the original text of the ordinance. However, the use of the following words at the very beginning of the Parking District Requirements hints of the possibility of some discretion: "*In General*, Required off-street parking must be: . . ." (p. 5). Interestingly, proposals for environmental protection in the Turtle Creek area included a self-administering approach for new construction and a flexible approach for existing structures. New construction in certain areas faces mandates for setbacks to "preserve a 'front yard' or private open space of a minimum of 50 feet from public property."[11] However, the summary proposed "that existing structures where possible be encouraged to conform to the above standards on a voluntary basis. . . ."[12]

Following all the "shalls", "musts", and mandatory requirements in the "Landscaping Regulations" are amendments to the Dallas Development Code that give the Board of Adjustment some discretionary duties. For example:

> (1) to hear and decide appeals from decisions of the building official which must be exercised in accordance with this chapter;

(2) to interpret the intent of the zoning district map when uncertainty exists because the actual physical features differ from those indicated on the zoning district map and when the rules set forth in the zoning district boundary regulations do not apply; . . .[13]

Indianapolis

It might appear that several cities we have examined by now have a design option administrative approach to the granting of exceptions and variances and the handling of special situations that may arise outside the usual codes and ordinances. It is difficult to assess just how much discretion (if any!) the evaluation body may have in reading the ordinances that pertain to these special circumstances. Consider the "Rules of Procedure" for the Metropolitan Development Commission (MDC) of Marion County/Indianapolis, Indiana, Article III, "Filing of Petitions for Zone Map Change, Approvals or Variances." The petitioner for variance "shall . . . file proposed detailed written findings of fact. Any other interested party may file proposed findings of fact. . . ."[14] The rules specify a series of procedures, including the public hearing before the hearing examiner.

Following the hearing, the examiner "shall announce whether his or her recommendation to the MDC shall be that the petition be approved, disapproved, or approved subject to any conditions, amendments or commitments by the petitioner."[15] Further, the hearing examiner is expected to comment on his or her findings. We cannot read between the lines, but we can surmise that some discretion may be used in the process. Appeals of the hearing examiner's decision are handled by the MDC in another public hearing.

Yet, when we examine Indianapolis's "Central Business District Zoning Ordinance" (August 1984), we find well-established limits for special exceptions: *"ONLY UPON THE METROPOLITAN BOARD'S DETERMINATION THAT* . . . (emphasis in the original, p. 21.). Then follow three statements setting the limits. Only if:

> not . . . injurious to the public health, safety, convenience or general welfare; . . . [it does] not injure or adversely affect the adjacent area or property value therein; [it] will be in harmony with the character of the district and land use authorized therein.[16]

There are other requirements as well. There is room for discretion, but it is circumscribed by built-in provisos.

Next we turn again to the Indianapolis Historic Preservation Commission's "Lockerbie Square Plan Design Standards." Our conclusions are more easily arrived at because of the following statements:

1. The commission "utilizes the design standards . . . as a guide in determining the appropriateness of projects within the Lockerbie Square Historic Area."
2. Property owners (and others) are to use these design standards as a guide when "developing a project within the Lockerbie Square Area."[17]

It is clear that discretion is used in judging projects in the Lockerbie Square Area. We'll call it a flexible administrative approach because there are quite complete guidelines to push the architect toward recommended procedures while avoiding "nonrecommended" or "inappropriate" design.

Irvine

Irvine has a form to cover any and all residential, landscaping, residential and tenant alteration, commercial or industrial proposals. The developer of a large area must submit a master plan for approval. There are directions for the building, fire, current planning, and engineering departments to follow in the code compliance review process. Detailed zoning maps of the entire city exist. One should not conclude that this is a completely cut-and-dried process—fill out the forms, pay the fees, submit the required materials, wait while the process grinds on (one to six weeks), obtain approval (with or without conditions) or denial.

Irvine has realized they cannot foresee all the possibilities. As in other cities, their ordinances make provision for lot-line adjustments, zoning changes, conditional use permits, park modification requests, and variances. Conditions may be attached to approved projects. And, of course, the procedure of appeal has to be spelled out. Appeals from decisions by the planning commission or subdivision committee are heard by the city council, who make discretionary decisions on matters brought before them. Yet, one may be sure that the council leans heavily on the recommendations of its planning staff and planning commission—and stays within the bounds of the ordinances.

There are, for example, three circumstances under which a park dedication modification may be requested. The Community Services Commission must examine all the information and materials the applicant presents and then make a recommendation of approval or denial to the Planning Commission. Very specific parameters are set; but the commission must make judgments on compliance and suitability of modifications proposed. We'll have to allow a tad of discretionary approach in Irvine's procedures.

Kansas City

Kansas City already has established strong controls of those elements deemed important to creating a quality environment. There are many "shalls" and "musts":

> Parking shall be provided within structured facilities . . . Each development shall provide for vehicular drop-off, direct access to garages . . .[18]

With regard to Special Review District, Main Street, we also find: "The site plan shall show clearly the design. . . ."[19] Indeed, special ordinances for individual areas of the city had become so numerous that in 1987 Kansas City's planning staff began work on "A City Plan for Urban Design and Development Policy," not to supplant individual plans but to coordinate them. We say, therefore, that Kansas City has a self-administering approach with many of its urban design efforts.

Again, however, we caution that Kansas City, too, has discovered a need for exercising some discretion as shown in presenting the powers and duties of the Board of Zoning Adjustment. Note how the language of the ordinances limits discretion. When hearing appeals from decisions of the codes administrator, the board "may make an order varying or modifying such rule or regulation." However, there must be "exceptional circumstances or surroundings [which] constitute a practical difficulty or unnecessary hardship."[20] Yet,

> the general purpose and intent of such rule or regulation may be preserved and the health, safety, convenience, comfort, prosperity, or general welfare . . . be secured and substantial justice be done by specific modification or variance of such rule or regulation to the specific case under consideration. . . . The Board shall impose such restrictions, terms and conditions governing use, yards, designs of buildings, time limitations, landscaping and other appropriate safeguards as may be in harmony with the purpose and intent of this Chapter. In no case shall the Board modify the requirements of this Chapter so as to substantially destroy or nullify these requirements.[21]

The redevelopment authority by ordinance is able to act more independently in the evaluation of projects, thereby showing some discretion in its approach. Controlled discretion also has been granted to the codes administrator "to approve changes to legal nonconformances under certain conditions."[22]

Lincoln

Lincoln's approach to design evaluation is not clear. As stated earlier, Lincoln's Urban Design Committee can only make recommendations concerning city projects, private projects to which the city has made financial contributions, or private projects located on city land. Evaluation of such projects takes place on an individual basis. The city has developed an urban design policy, but its administration is hampered by present law. Lincoln is still trying to promote urban design and preservation by annual awards for "good urban design . . . completed in the last year, one for a project from the private sector and one from the public sector."[23]

Minneapolis

With a complete zoning code and planning for special districts already in place, we immediately can conclude that Minneapolis has a design option approach to the design evaluation process. The rules and regulations are there to guide the architect in compliance. The evaluation team's main task, then, is to advise and explain the options to the architect. However, the architect must be prepared to cope with the city policy "to maximize citizen involvement in decisions which affect City programs or policies."[24] A request for changes or a conditional use may trigger a response tempered with some discretion by the zoning administrator's office and the planning staff in making recommendations to the planning commission and the city council.

Portland

Portland's decisions to establish special districts (Z, Downtown Zone; D, Design Zone; Historic Districts; etc.) changed the complexion of design evaluation in the city. Outside these zones, evaluation is design option oriented; the rules are there for the architect to follow. However, within each of the special districts, discretionary evaluation is possible and is Portland's response to the special needs of each district. The proven value of flexibility in regulations has led Portland to expand the boundaries of the area to be covered by the Downtown Plan. This new plan, which took effect in July 1988, has not yet extended the design guidelines from the Downtown Plan, but it is a recognition of the expansive nature of downtown activities necessitating closer scrutiny of housing needs and coordinated development. The Bureau of Planning is to administer the new plan.

San Diego

San Diego has attempted to address special needs in varying areas of the city by overlay zones which add requirements to the basic underlying code/zone of each area. Urban design was recognized as a particular need in all areas. We find, for example, an "Urban Design Program and Streetscape Design Manual" for Centre City, a concept soon to be applied beyond the redevelopment area to all parts of the city on a community-by-community basis.

> This expansion of design evaluation includes the following objective: The project review and permit issuance process should be as expeditious, predictable, and equitable as possible. Precise standards and guidelines coupled with modifications to the discretionary permit process and a greater emphasis on ministerial permit processing will be required.[25]

Among the recommendations are creation of urban design elements for each community plan, review and revision of development criteria, increased enforcement of regulations, and "tailored zoning" appropriate to each community.[26] It would appear that San Diego wants to continue its design option approach, allowing only limited discretion in evaluation. While we might say that the building inspector and planning director exert discretionary power in approving minor planning and design matters, this, too, is an activity that proceeds in a highly organized fashion within clearly defined parameters.

San Francisco

The Planning Commission in San Francisco makes decisions on project approval or rejection after receiving input from the staff of San Francisco's Planning Department, advice from the Architectural Review Panel, and the to-be-expected (especially in San Francisco!) comment from the public. The discussion in Chapter 1 concerning San Francisco's office limitation program has illustrated the existence of extensive regulations in the city. Yet, San Francisco, a city that prides itself on individuality and ambience, has made a place for discretion in the application of its ordinances. Further, the city encourages and relies on informal sessions between staff and architect to resolve differences and allow speedier processing of applications at lower cost.

Whether these stringent measures really do encourage San Francisco's ambience is not certain. If, indeed, San Francisco reaches the goal of having " '. . . almost everyone . . . within 900 feet (approximately 2 blocks) of a publicly accessible space in which to sit, eat a brown-bag lunch, and people watch,' "[27] the citizens may more readily accept rigorous self-administered controls. So regulation marches on. In March 1988, the Board of Supervisors "approved a five-month freeze on the demolition of single-family homes."[28] What is the likelihood of such a provision continuing?

Seattle

Seattle does have a Design Commission, but it is empowered only to make recommendations to city staff and city council on city capital projects. Its power, therefore, is limited; it proceeds within the bounds of ordinances. But the city's capital projects have been quite exemplary in any case, this despite the city's being both applicant and evaluator. The commission makes recommendations but cannot force their implementation. It is therefore not quite possible to identify Seattle with one of the four approaches.

When we examine the general special districts, we find a great variance in the evaluation of proposed projects. This probably has been caused by the differing natures of the special districts. The enabling legislation for special districts allows each to set its own standards. For example, in the Pike Place Market Historical District there is a Historical Commission advised by a District Design Review Committee. Evaluation is generally confined to design concerns, and environmental impact and planning matters are within the purview of the city staff. The city passed ordinances

> for control of changes and modifications in the Pike Place Market Historical District. . . . [The guidelines] are to help preserve and improve the District. . . . [They] are to be interpreted liberally; they should not prevent spontaneous development nor force uneconomic uses or changes.[29]

Yet, the city warns that the guidelines

> are . . . based upon and drawn from the Ordinance. . . . The Commission is to pass on all applications for building permits and Certificates of Approval involving demolishing, building, renovating, altering, modifying, changing, improving and even painting, as well as changes in use within the seven-acre District.[30]

The picture is entirely different in the Columbia City Landmark District with its Application Review Committee. The guidelines are two and one-half pages long, with the first page devoted to a "Statement of Intent." There also are "Guidelines/General" and about a page of "Guidelines/Specific." Signage seems to be the main concern, with but three guidelines devoted to facades, relationship of buildings to public areas, and preservation of the "integrity of structure, form and decoration."[31]

Vail

Design evaluation in Vail provides an interesting and somewhat confusing mix of flexible and design option guidelines. It would appear that Vail has attempted to provide creative opportunities with their discretionary guidelines and mandatory requirements for those items deemed essential to the preservation of Vail's unique atmosphere. There is, for example, little give in permitted and conditional uses allowed in Vail Village. On the other hand, Vail is more flexible with regard to overall objectives such as preserving land forms and features and the pedestrian atmosphere in Vail Village. "Should" and "may" introduce those guidelines.

The "shalls" outweigh the "shoulds." A project application can become quite lengthy when an architect is attempting to meet all the requirements.

The statement in Section 18.54.040.A of the *Zoning Title,* "Materials to be submitted/procedures," hints of possible complexities in the process: "Topics of discussion shall include but [are] not limited to . . ."

2.3 THE COMMON GROUND

Due to the differences among evaluation bodies evident in the study of our 12 cities, architects must educate themselves not only on the immediate concerns of the project but also on the way in which they must deal with the review body. A great deal of emphasis is placed on justification of the architectural concept, leading perhaps to more mundane design solutions. Architects by nature think spatially rather than verbally. The discrepancy between the utilitarian terms that must be used for evaluation boards to understand and the design vocabulary of the architect creates a schism in communication between the parties involved.

While a discretionary evaluation process follows fewer written rules and regulations, it is a subjective exercise dependent upon the composition of its evaluation team. Freedom of design is quite extensive through the development phase, but that freedom is severely diminished once the evaluating body applies its discretion. On the other hand, the self-administering system leaves very little room for the subjective nature of certain design aspects. A recipe for design is given with few chances for innovation, a process based on compliance. The design option approach seems to come closer to striking a balance between given requirements and the individuality of the project's design.

We must judge the success and failure of the reviewing bodies in terms of the design evaluation process itself. Any inadequacies must be recognized as an outgrowth of the quasi-institutionality that encompasses the evaluation body, not the individual members themselves. The format of the test needs to be reconsidered before we get rid of those who are doing the grading. The makeup of the evaluation body itself and its relative position within the overall framework of civic structure is examined in the next chapter.

REFERENCE NOTES

1. Thomas Nally, "Design Review, Alternative Models of Administration" (M.Arch. A.S./M.C.P. thesis, MIT, 1977); Hamid Shirvani, *Urban Design Review* (Chicago: Planners Press, 1981).
2. City of Baltimore, Baltimore City Department of Housing and Community Development, "Inner Harbor Project I Renewal Plan," originally approved June 15, 1967, with amendments through May 8, 1985, 6.

3. Ibid., 21.
4. Ibid., 10.
5. Ibid.
6. City of Baltimore, "Design Advisory Panel Guidelines," revised, October 1983, 1.
7. Ibid.
8. City of Baltimore, Baltimore City Commission for Historical and Architectural Preservation, "Historic Preservation Guidelines," n.d., Section A.
9. Ibid.
10. City of Dallas, Department of Planning and Development, "Landmark Preservation Incentives for the City of Dallas Central Business District," Publication No. 83-1076, n.d., 1.
11. City of Dallas, Department of Urban Planning, "Turtle Creek Environmental Corridor Summary," May 1974 (and revised), 4.
12. Ibid., 5.
13. City of Dallas, *Ordinance 18968*, amending Chapter 51 DALLAS DEVEL-OPMENT CODE (as amended), "Landscaping Regulations," December 11, 1985, 16.
14. Metropolitan Development Commission of Marion County/Indianapolis, Indiana, Article III, "Filing of Petitions for Zone Map Change, Approvals or Variances," November 5, 1986, 7.
15. Ibid., 23.
16. Marion County, Department of Metropolitan Development, Division of Development Services, "Central Business District Zoning Ordinance, Recommendation," II.2.05.A.1.a, Docket Numbers: Original 64-AO-1 and amending 01-AO-4, August 1984, 21.
17. City of Indianapolis, Indianapolis Historic Preservation Commission, "Lockerbie Square Plan, Design Standards," January 1987, D1.
18. City of Kansas City, "Board of Trade Urban Renewal Plan," September 24, 1986, 14.
19. City of Kansas City, City Development Department, Planning Division, "Rules and Regulations for Implementing Ordinance 59380, Main Street Design Review Committee," May 19, 1987, 3, in "Special Review District Main Street," a folder to guide applicants through the Main Street Special Design Review Process, August 1, 1987.
20. City of Kansas City, *Zoning Ordinance*, 39.3000.I.C, "Powers and Duties of the Board of Adjustment," January 1987, 143
21. Ibid.
22. Ibid., 60825, "Amending Chapter 39 by repealing Section 39.230 and enacting in lieu a new section of like number," August 20, 1987, 1.
23. "Lincoln-Lancaster County Comprehensive Plan," 1985, 220.
24. City of Minneapolis, City Planning Commission, "City Planning Commission," October 16, 1979, with corrections February 18, 1988, 3.
25. City of San Diego, City Planning Department, "Urban Design Program," Planning Report No. 85-152, April 10, 1985, 11-12.
26. Ibid., 1-2.

27. George Williams, in "Make No Little Dreams," Frank Viviano and Sharon Silva, *TWA Ambassador* (January 1986):58.

28. Gerald D. Adams, "San Francisco Develops Tough Stance on Growth," *Minneapolis Star Tribune* (March 5, 1988): 3R.

29. City of Seattle, "Pike Place Market Historical Commission Guidelines," adopted November 13, 1980, and revised June 1982, 1.

30. Ibid.

31. City of Seattle, "The Columbia City Landmark District," 1979, 12.

Chapter 3

FRAMEWORK AND ACTORS

In this chapter we will examine the framework and actors involved in the evaluation of the architecture of the city, in terms of both the composition of the team and its organizational structure. In investigating both the knowledge and qualifications of the evaluation body and its public representations as well as the relationship of the body to the city organization, we can begin to see the interplay of public architecture with other factors in the overall decision-making process of the city.

Three basic definitions can be used to describe the formal structure of the evaluation team in most cities: (1) team composed exclusively of professional designers (architects, landscape architects, and urban planners); (2) team composed of both professional designers and nondesigners (citizens); and (3) team composed exclusively of nondesigners. In all of the above combinations, the members, both designers and nondesigners, can be staff members of a city agency and/or citizens.

A close look at the 12 cities studied here will offer us some issues of concern in regard to each of the above-mentioned formal evaluation structures.

3.1 CASE STUDIES

In the 12 cities studied, the organizational location of the design evaluation team can be explained in one of three ways. Perhaps it is outside the city organization as an independent body advisory to the mayor or city council. Another option is having the design evaluation team outside of the city organization and advisory to the planning department staff rather than to the political decision makers. Third, the design evaluation team may be within the city organization as a part of the planning department; that is, the evaluators are on the planning department staff itself. As we discuss the structure and organization of design evaluation teams, we will soon discover that there often is a variety of approaches within a city reflecting a variety of public interests.

Baltimore

One of Baltimore's emphases, for example, is historical and architectural preservation. The Commission on Historical and Architectural Preservation, CHAP, draws its members from a number of different professions and from the citizenry. There are to be representatives from the boards of trustees of the Municipal Museum of Baltimore and the Walter Art Gallery, from the Council of the Maryland Historical Society, and from city council. Also to be included are a practicing architect and a member of the history faculty from a college or university or an individual engaged in a nonprofit organization with historic interest. Citizens interested in civic improvement fill the last four positions on CHAP, forming an 11-member board appointed by the mayor and city council for five-year staggered terms. Renomination and reappointment to CHAP are possible.

CHAP's recommendations on new construction, demolition, or renovation projects including repainting, cleaning of masonry, and repair and replacement of exterior aspects of structures are forwarded to the city council. The teeth in CHAP's requirements are the necessity of obtaining a Notice to Proceed prior to beginning a project. The City of Baltimore and the Charles Center Redevelopment Authority have a Design Advisory Panel (DAP) and an Architectural Review Board (ARB), respectively. DAP deals solely with projects that include some public financing, while ARB evaluates downtown urban renewal projects. DAP is advisory to the housing commissioner in the Department of Community Development and ultimately to the planning commission and the mayor's office. ARB reports to the Charles Center Housing Authority. Its power is limited to recommendations.

Previously we have mentioned Baltimore's growth into a city of neighborhoods. The creation of a Neighborhood Progress Administration is a reflection of this tendency. Each neighborhood has a community association made up of interested citizens who live and/or work there. A 1987 directory lists 23 city-wide groups, 26 umbrella organizations representing several neighborhoods and/or interests, and more than 200 citizen groups that bear names showing neighborhood concerns: West Arlington Merchants Association, South Baltimore Improvement Committee, Ramblewood Community Association, Alba Neighborhood Association, Bay View Civic Association, etc. Baltimore's response to this consciousness of neighborhood was to divide the city into 38 planning areas, with six planners separately assigned to districts made up of several planning areas. The neighborhood organizations are advisory on matters of design and planning in their own areas. Note that these organizations exist in addition to the groups in historical districts. The citizen participation is extensive and most noteworthy.

Each of Baltimore's urban renewal areas has established design standards which developers must meet. For example, in the Urban Renewal Plan of the

Charles/North Revitalization Area, we find eight pages devoted to "Review of Developer's Plans." Expressed is an interest in achieving

> harmonious development of the project area. Such review and approval shall take into consideration, but shall not be limited to, the suitability of the plan, architectural treatment, building plans, elevations, materials and colors, construction details, access, parking, loading, landscaping, sidewalks and the harmony of the plans with the surroundings.[1]

Because of the complexity of Baltimore's regulations and the maze of design review and citizen organizations, a nonprofit organization, the Neighborhood Design Center of Baltimore/D.C., provides advice on architectural and design matters and assistance to groups evaluating design proposals.

Dallas

In Dallas, all projects must undergo careful scrutiny for compliance with city codes, but only projects in special districts (e.g., West End Historical District, Central Business District, and Market District) must submit to design evaluation. However, landscaping and signage requirements are city-wide at present and would receive close attention. As in Baltimore, Dallas wants to encourage community participation and citizen input into neighborhood design decisions. Therefore, if there is a neighborhood design committee

> established in accordance with the . . . guidelines, the director [of planning] shall consult with the committee in a timely manner during the review process to apprise himself of community concerns, and to receive additional input in resolving problems of ambiguity.[2]

Such a neighborhood design committee could wield considerable influence on a director of planning.

The City Plan Commission, Dallas Park Board, Landmark Committee, and Sign Ordinance Review Committee all have some design evaluation responsibilities. The city council or a council committee appoint the members of these groups, and all have specific legally mandated roles to play. Note, however, that single homes and duplexes are exempt from landscape review in planned districts, because the district ordinance applies rather than the city-wide regulations. We will discuss Dallas's sign ordinance later.

Serving outside the city organization is the Urban Design Task Force (UDTF). The city manager makes annual appointments to this group, usually from a list of nominees suggested by the chairman of city council. Generally, the membership includes architects, planners, landscape architects, and engineers. The power of UDTF is limited to advising the city manager on urban design concerns and providing an interdepartmental overview of programs and projects.

It is the City Plan Commission that gives final approval to projects on the basis of design and code compliance. This commission has 15 members who serve two-year terms. Each of the 12 city council members appoints a person to the commission, and there are three at-large members. Present (1988) membership reflects a broad representation of Dallas's citizens. There are three attorneys, a developer, the owner of a paint manufacturing company, a banker, a real estate investor, a real estate broker, two homemakers, an architect, a public relations consultant, the deputy director of the Environmental Planning Division, a USAF Regional Civil Engineering representative, and the senior administrative assistant to the county commissioners. It is important that most of these individuals have lived in Dallas for ten or more years, and three are natives.

At present, Dallas has a district focus to its design evaluation, and its planned districts have been quite varied and successful. Official recognition has been given to the Dallas Arts District, the Near Eastside Development District, and the Oak Lawn Special District (among others) since 1981. What we must ask is if these successes make Dallas more design-conscious city-wide.

Indianapolis

Design evaluation in Indianapolis appears to be a markedly formalized function with some citizen representation on the Metropolitan Design Commission (MDC). The city's Department of Metropolitan Development (DMD) and the MDC both have ordinance-mandated design evaluation functions. Remembering the rather complex intertwinement of Indianapolis and Marion County governments, it is not surprising that the city/county council appoints three members to the MDC; the Marion County commissioners, two; and the mayor, four members. Terms are for two years, and the 1988 MDC was diverse, with attorneys and other professionals and homemakers among the membership. The MDC is not specifically an evaluation board; ordinances provide for the MDC to function as the Metropolitan Board of Zoning Appeal as well as an advisory body giving advice and recommendations to the city/county council on design and planning matters.

When city/county government began close cooperation in 1970 with Unigov, they created the DMD and gave it extensive powers in design and planning matters. Design approval is one of their duties, and three staff members in the Division of Planning oversee urban design. They then advise the Division of Development Services (DDS) concerning the design quality of a proposed project, while other sections of the DMD evaluate other project aspects. Additionally, the Indianapolis Historic Preservation Commission, a part of DMD, provides assistance to neighborhood groups who are trying to establish historic areas. The guidelines for development and rehabilitation are set in Indianapolis's code and are consequently quite enforceable. Strong neighborhood groups exist in some subareas; other subareas lack active citizenry.

Irvine

Community organizations have been encouraged by The Irvine Company, and their function in design evaluation is recognized by the City of Irvine, too. Let us refer to Westpark again. Westpark Maintenance District, a legally constituted body, exercises architectural and thematic control as mandated by its covenant within the framework of company and city mandates. Smaller areas within Westpark have project associations to further assure continuity of design, construction, and repair. Approval (or disapproval) of plans is the responsibility of Westpark's Architectural Committee. This all is a manifestation of The Irvine Company's delegated design review control after developers create communities within the company's prescribed standards.

Understand that approval must also come from the city's exercising zoning and code restrictions. The city planning staff makes design (and other) recommendations to the City Planning Commission, whose members are appointed by individual council members and serve one year or as long as the council member himself/herself serves. Reappointment is possible. The 1988 City Planning Commission included an architect, a person from the County Housing Department, an attorney, and a journalist.

Within the Community Development Department, the professional staff oversees city projects and the design and technical aspects of city and private projects. Emphasis is on technical matters because of the strong influence of The Irvine Company and citizen groups on design and architectural concerns. A special Community Urban Design Advisory Committee, composed of 11 members, assisted the council in the framing of the 1977 Urban Design Implementation Plan. The code provides that the council or the planning commission may appoint such citizen committees to advise them.

Kansas City

Citizens appointed by the mayor serve on "more than 100 boards and commissions created by the city charter or ordinance to advise the city council and city departments on matters involving Kansas City."[3] The plan commission is no exception. The eight members of the commission typically have some expertise in land-use matters. At the time of this writing, an architect, attorneys, neighborhood leaders, and realtors were serving on the commission, with one vacancy waiting to be filled. The plan commission is a policy-making board that hears most development issues and makes recommendations to the council on design and other matters. Members of the plan commission also serve on the Board of Adjustment.

The City Development Department Planning Division provides professional support to the plan commission and suggests approvals, denials, and conditional approvals, particularly on design issues. An unusual part of the CDD is the Business Assistance Center, which since 1983 has helped "developers and builders get their projects through the local government process."[4] The Development Management Division in the CDD evaluates the plans submitted in the building permit process, advises the plan commission, and provides support staff for the Board of Zoning Adjustment and city council. Very little of their work specifically involves evaluation of urban design. However, they do have an urban design consultant on retainer. Two other appointed commissions are the Municipal Art Commission (MAC) and the Landmark Commission (LC). MAC "authorizes all plans for structures built on or extending over public property [and] initiates design projects."[5] Some overlap occurs because the chairperson of the plan commission also serves on MAC and on the Trafficways Commission, where some design matters receive attention.

Kansas City's Redevelopment Authority began with strong business ties as the Kansas City Corporation for Independent Development in 1977. The authority operates outside city government. Its staff includes designers and planners who evaluate plans in cooperation with the City Planning Division and the Landmark Commission. This latter commission also informally evaluates projects and keeps tabs on design matters in designated historic areas. The LC also helps neighborhood groups attain district or individual building historic status.

Lincoln

Planning commission members in Lincoln serve six-year terms in contrast to the much shorter tenures seen in the previously discussed cities. The citizen membership has a broad background: three attorneys, a newspaper circulation manager, a teacher, a union representative, a planning professional, a banker, and a doctor. They are advisory to the city council.

Since 1981, Lincoln has had an Urban Design Review Committee authorized by city ordinance which mandates that

> the committee shall have seven members appointed by the mayor with the approval of the city council. Insofar as practicable, all members of the committee shall be competent in matters of design, representative of the community, and should include individuals with a demonstrated interest or education in matters of urban design.[6]

The 1988 members included a landscape architect, a private planner, an artist, a banker, a real estate developer, and a planning staff representative. The chairperson is to be a practicing architect. Terms are for three years. The committee's role is solely advisory to all parts of city government, and their concern encompasses matters on a city- or county-wide, neighborhood, or individual project scale.

A traditional historical preservation commission is at work in Lincoln. Both professionals and citizens serve on the commission. Present members include a historian, two architects, a landscape architect, a realtor, and two citizens. A 1985 attempt to merge this commission with the Urban Design Review Committee failed.

Minneapolis

We have mentioned previously that Minneapolis's successes in design have come despite a lack of coordinated design evaluation. Involved are the City Planning Department, the City Planning Commission, the city council, the zoning administrator, and the Committee on Urban Environment (CUE). The City Planning Department provides staff support to the City Planning Commission, the Board of Adjustment, and CUE. The building permit process ends in the City Planning Department with issuance or denial or a conditional permit.

Terms of the planning commission members are two years. Four of the nine members are appointed by the mayor and approved by the council. Four other members represent Minneapolis's city council, the Hennepin County Board of Commissioners, the Park and Recreation Board, and the Board of Education. The ninth member is the mayor or the mayor's delegated representative. Except for the city employees already receiving salaries, the members are paid for each official meeting. The planning commission's recommendations on projects are sent to the city council. They and the zoning administrator take on the usual roles of respectively giving final approval to project proposals and issuing a building permit—if all aspects of the proposal are in proper order.

CUE has 27 members, an executive committee, and four standing committees. Once again, we find representatives from many branches of city government and two aldermen. Eight members are appointed by the mayor and nine by the president of city council. Special task forces take on investigations of issues cited by the executive committee, mayor, city council, and citizen groups. CUE's by-laws include the following "duties":

> . . . 3. Support highest design standards in all public and private architecture and environmental improvements. . . . 5. Upon request, advise the City Council, and the Boards, Commissions, officials of the City and private enterprise with respect to plans and actions which could affect or involve the purposes for which the Committee is established.[7]

CUE does not sit idly by waiting to be asked; its members are busy being visible in the community by sponsoring awards for the improvement of neighborhood environments and holding a Blooming Boulevard Contest. In 1987, their focus was the greening of downtown Minneapolis. CUE's literature encourages citizens to become involved in improving the urban environment in Minneapolis. With this stimulus, it is no wonder that the City of Minneapolis created a Riverfront Recreation, Cultural, and Entertainment Committee which met from October 1986 through April 1987. Their report was referred to the Riverfront Technical Advisory Committee as "the next step toward redevelopment of the central riverfront as a premier public amenity. . . ."[8]

Portland

Portland has emphasized urban design in the downtown area, but organizing urban design efforts has become quite complex, with base zones, special districts, and overlay zones. Consider, for example, the C1 Commercial Zone where its base zone requirements are modified by two overlay zones, the Z Downtown Development Zone and the D Design Zone. The Bureau of Planning staff oversees design matters in C1, but the regulations of design and landmarks commissions must be followed. The city council has the ultimate authority for design (and planning) decisions.

Our interest focuses on the D Design Zone, which overlays all downtown base zones and certain areas beyond downtown. The design criteria here are most stringent because they must preserve and enhance the best aspects of Portland. A particular emphasis is projects funded with public monies. The planning director and the design commission evaluate all permit requests. The planning bureau handles review and approval for minor projects, while the design commission must handle the major projects.

There are seven persons on the design commission appointed by the mayor with council confirmation. Portland seeks persons with specific qualifications: a citizen "at-large;" four members with design, planning, engineering, financing, construction or land development, or legal experience; one representative of the planning commission; and one person from the Metropolitan Arts Commission. They serve four-year terms (no more than two consecutively) and do not need to reside in Portland. The 1988 members included an architect, landscape architect, and designer; a realtor; a citizen activist; a developer; and a land-use attorney. The design commission is advisory to the city council.

San Diego

San Diego's Planning Department bears most of the responsibility for evaluation of urban design. The city's commitment to improving urban design aids in the enforcement of standards. The public and developers both know what to expect. It has been possible for the city to include an urban design section in its planning department. They maintain a constant program of evaluation of the city's environment so that they are able to propose changes and effectively review the urban design aspects of a proposed project. Other sections of the planning department and other city departments share in evaluation responsibilities. Planning Director Michael Stepner has stressed that San Diego's Planning Department "has been moving forward to a full Urban Design Program; albeit, incrementally."[9]

San Diego goes beyond bricks and mortar and tries to enhance livability with a seven-member Quality of Life Board. They are to "provide expertise from the academic and business communities to advise Mayor and City Council on policies and actions which affect the quality of life in San Diego [and] maintain a Science Resource Panel to assist in its work."[10] San Diego also has two planned district boards, for Old San Diego and La Jolla Shores. Design evaluation is an important part of these citizens' work, and they are advisory to the planning commission and council. As in other cities, the redevelopment authorities in San Diego proceed somewhat independently of city mandates. I do not mean to imply they do not have to meet code requirements; rather I am referring to the power given by the city council to evaluate design independently "to ensure that they [development proposals] meet design criteria and other public objectives."[11]

Forty-five recognized community planning areas in San Diego have organized citizen volunteers to review proposals in their neighborhoods and advise the planning department of their concerns. Outside the city government, and not even mayorally appointed, these groups are able to exert considerable influence, both individually and as a group. The "Community Planner's Committee" is an informal organization of the chairpersons of the many neighborhood groups who review and evaluate proposals city-wide. They even are recognized on the "Planning Department Functional Organizational Chart" (p. 6). The Community Planning Division "provide[s] staff support to the Community Planners Committee."

Finally, the Gaslamp Quarter Council and the Centre City Advisory Committee, both citizen design evaluation groups, play important parts in shaping new ordinances and in evaluating proposed projects. Citizens with design concerns have formed interest groups to press their ideas with the city's government; their vocal concerns have led the city to establish more urban design requirements and a city-wide landscaping plan.

San Francisco

Recall that San Francisco's Planning Department staff has retained three independent architects to assist with evaluation of projects seeking approval within the city's strict office space limitations. They form an Architectural

Review Committee, and their findings aid the planning staff in making recommendations to the planning commission, which seeks the opinion of staff before making decisions on the validity of proposals brought before it. The 1988 planning commission members included an investment and finance consultant, a dentist, a neighborhood activist, and a businesswoman. The city architect and the director of planning and development for the Public Utility Commission are ex officio members.

The East Slope Building Review Board, the Northwest Bernal Neighborhood Building Review Board, and the Union Street Association all function as design evaluators in their particular areas. The Planning Commission uses their input as well. The Landmarks Preservation Board (LPB), in place since 1967, has nine members and the usual historic district responsibilities. Standards for buildings and areas are fairly well established, and within that framework the LPB must exercise design evaluation.

Seattle

As in most other cities, Seattle's Planning Commission makes recommendations on various proposals to the city council. Their broad approach precludes specific design evaluation action but sets a proper stage for it. There are 15 members on the planning commission, and it is a mixed group of professionals and citizens. In contrast, the design commission makes recommendations on environmental and design aspects of proposals for city projects. Its members have been active, trying to positively influence plans for city parks, Seattle Center renovations, etc. The design commission is an eight-member board with specially qualified persons serving: two architects, one urban planner, one landscape architect, two engineers, one fine artist, and one lay person. At present, the lay person is an architect! The city council is not legally bound to follow the design commission's recommendations.

Special district review boards and commissions fulfill a particular need in Seattle's design evaluation program. Consider the Pike Place Market Historical Commission, charged with preserving and improving the district with guidelines "designed to be sensitive to its unique characteristics."[12] The commission has twelve members appointed by the mayor and confirmed by council. They serve three-year terms with reappointment allowed for a second term only.

In a further refinement not found in other cities, there is a subcommittee, the District Design Review Committee, on which three commission members serve rotating one-year terms. This committee has a predesign conference with a developer; depending on the committee's success in bringing about desired changes in a proposed plan, they will recommend approval or denial of the project to the full commission. Commission recommendations go to the Department of Construction and Land Use. The Pioneer Square Preservation District Commission has nine members, again mayorally appointed and confirmed by council. Again, their background is specified: one historian (or architectural historian), one human services representative, two architects, two property owners, one retail business owner, one attorney, and one member at-large. The current at-large member is an attorney. In both these districts, concurrent reviews by the particular district commission and the design committee are possible if a city project is involved.

Vail

Vail has a four-person planning staff and has followed a practice of having private consultants to assist in drawing up design guidelines, in designing public projects, and in evaluating private proposals. The Vail Town Council appoints the five-member Design Review Board, with one member representing the Planning and Environmental Commission on a three-month rotating basis. Currently, the membership includes a real estate person, a painting contractor, and two architects. No doubt to the envy of their counterparts in other cities, Vail's Design Review Board makes final decisions on design matters. However, the applicant may appeal a decision to Vail's Town Council.

The town and its citizenry must feel comfortable with their design control mechanisms and with their planning staff to give the Design Review Board so much power. Both guidelines and ordinances direct the design evaluation process. It should be mentioned, however, that design evaluation is but part of the review process. Vail also requires strict review by the Planning and Environmental Commission.

3.2 THE COMMON GROUND

The preceding examination of the 12 cities' structure and the makeup of their evaluation teams brings up several questions, the most fundamental of which is whether or not an evaluation team is a group of experts with the task of giving advice to the political decision makers. Or is it a political advocacy group of developers, builders, business members, neighborhood associations, or other politically interested parties? In the latter case, the role of the team member as "politician" or "technician" is unclear; therefore, the guidelines, standards, and criteria under the evaluation process are ambiguous. The question of interests served through the review board becomes even more problematic when one considers the makeup of the team. As we have seen, most cities have a combination of both professional designers and nondesigners, the citizens.

While many disciplines are recognized and represented in the membership of the evaluation teams studied, the participants are given these positions generally through appointment by city council members or the mayor, and in the case of Irvine, by the development company (The Irvine Company) itself. This is usually the case whether the review board works within or outside a city's government. Therein lies the danger of design evaluation becoming a political issue. There is the possibility of loyalty to political interest rather than allegiance to quality architecture of the city. Once certain policy trends are adopted or financial pressures acknowledged, a change in these policies can be used to judge the political performance of those responsible for implementing that change. The status quo becomes the safest route to follow.

I wish to make it clear that I am not challenging the democratic nature of this group dynamic. On the contrary, my criticism is that in a true democratic sense, the evaluation team should be composed of both citizens and designers; but the role of the designer and the city should be in part the education of nondesigners and citizens. This would encourage informed decisions and lead the team toward the overall goal of improving the architecture of the city as opposed to serving individual interests.

Finally, as it has been clearly demonstrated through the various cases, there is fragmentation of architecture of the city either by district focus (downtown, x neighborhood, y historic district, etc.) or by economic focus (residential, commercial, etc.). It is understandable that some districts or areas in various cities have a special historic or significant character that necessitates special guidelines and treatment; however, the result of this fragmentation into different ambitions and goals has created a city of islands, each with its own agenda.

The missing ingredient is coherence in discourse on the architecture of the city, a method of cultivating diversity and nourishing the reality of urban texture. Among the cities studied here, San Diego is the only city that is truly championing this consideration. Again, by raising this question, I am not alluding to the idea of an overall master plan for design. Rather, I am looking for a comprehensive understanding of the totality of existing structure of the city as well as its historical layer as a basis for development of guidelines and as an educational tool for decision making within the evaluation team. San Diego has come the closest to forming such a structure.

REFERENCE NOTES

1. City of Baltimore, Department of Housing and Community Development, "Urban Renewal Plan, Charles/North Revitalization Area," originally approved October 25, 1982, and amended May 21, 1984, and April 16, 1987, 7.

2. City of Dallas, Department of Planning, "Draft of an Ordinance Amending Ordinance No. 18312 . . . [for] Planned Development District No. 178," December 13, 1985, 7.

3. City of Kansas City, Public Information Office, "Your Kansas City Government," June 1987, 1.

4. Ibid., 14.

5. Ibid., 16.

6. City of Lincoln, Municipal Ordinance 13092, January 1981.

7. City of Minneapolis, "By-laws of CUE," February 9, 1968 (revised October 22, 1980), Article II, 1.

8. City of Minneapolis, Riverfront Recreation, Entertainment and Cultural Committee, "Report to the City of Minneapolis," May 1987, Letter of Transmittal.

9. Michael Stepner, letter to Dr. Robert Freilich, January 19, 1988.

10. Ibid.

11. Gerald M. Trimble and Stuart L. Rogel, "Horton Plaza: Codevelopment Rebuilds Downtown Excitement," *Urban Land* (July 1983):19.

12. City of Seattle, Pike Place Market Historical Commission, "Guidelines," 1987, 2.

Chapter 4

CONTEXT

Having examined the categories of public evaluation, the bureaucratic processes through which they are implemented, and the organization of those who act within this framework, let us now turn to a discussion of the context of public architecture. For our purposes, we define context as the boundary and nature of the means by which the architecture of the city is achieved. The most common means for this purpose have been the "guidelines."

What are "guidelines," and what is their structure? What is the basis for the development of such guidelines? These questions will form the discussion in this chapter. We will begin with a definition of guidelines; then we will examine the types of guidelines presently in practice. Finally, we will outline their fundamental problems and shortcomings.

4.1 GUIDELINES

The idea behind architectural design guidelines as well as design guidelines in general grew out of classical zoning and other traditional methods of land-use and building regulation. The early zoning ordinances prescribed what was *not* to be done, attempting to avoid the worst case and leaving a lot of gray area in between. Further development of zoning led the architects, planners, and legislators to believe that the regulations, in fact, could be a prescriptive tool rather than a method of prohibition, guiding development in a more positive sense and operating as a mechanism to promote quality rather than solely controlling the negative consequences. As a response, the notion of "guidelines" came into existence sometime in the 1960s to offer an ameliorative approach. Soon afterward, it was realized that not each and every architectural and design guideline can or should be legislated. Accordingly, some guidelines were added to cities' zoning, and other alternatives were developed as nonregulative and supplementary to the ordinances. Now, after several decades of development and widespread use of guidelines, they are becoming a common and accepted tool in many cities. Most of the cities we have studied in this book employ some kind of design guidelines.

The nature of the guidelines reveals a great deal about the attitude of the city organization toward architecture and the urban experience. The tendency in creating guidelines is toward either a prescriptive, interpretive approach that is predetermined, or the opposite, the performance, goal-oriented approach based on the realization of objectives that can be quantified. The two types of guidelines tend to pertain to different aspects of architecture and design. The prescriptive guidelines preserve a certain style and character, while the performance guidelines maintain a functional standard. These are extremes, and the cities discussed may use modified versions or a combination of the two.

Prescriptive guidelines lay down a set of possibilities for the content of architecture and design. The measure of the prescribed format is largely qualitative, descriptive, and consequently subjective by nature. Their influence is principally in the realm of style and is rooted in the traditional notions of compliance within the fabric of the city. It follows that this type of standard is used in the guidelines of historic districts. Building materials, signage, and colors are often dictated through the direction of the guidelines as well as building height, setbacks, and projections. In this approach the solutions are given without necessarily stating the goal.

The performance guidelines, on the other hand, do not specifically describe the solution but rather outline the described result. It is up to the designer/architect to achieve it in the design details. The emphasis is placed on innovation through fulfillment of a measurable goal rather than compliance with a predetermined solution. Therefore, the design evaluators carefully calculate the results of a project. If that project meets the given level of traffic or sewerage, for example, the design evaluators confirm that the project has been designed to their requirements. If not, it is then up to the architects to go back and modify the design to meet those specific requirements. The particular disposition toward design methodology of the professional can, however, be dictated, in some cases, through the language of this otherwise objective type of guideline; the categories of style and the codification of elements are not the primary concerns to be regulated.

Another example would be a requirement that window openings should be large enough to produce a 2 percent daylight factor within every room. This is a performance guideline; it does not prescribe the measurements of the window opening, nor does it say where those window openings should be. However, it does require that inside the spaces there must be a 2 percent daylight factor. The rest is left to the architect's creativity. While the performance-based guidelines foster innovative solutions in obtaining a goal, the goals themselves are for the most part unquestioned once they reach the status of city policy. The preceding examples are quite objective, but we will see later how these guidelines can also be quite descriptive in their application.

When looking at a contemporary city, we find a curious mixture of the modern and the premodern concept of urban space. The traditional premodern urban fabric was essentially an interrelated series of spaces connecting the public and private sectors. The building solids defined the voids, and these voids took precedence over the solids. The modern fabric of the city is in the opposite condition, with the solids existing in space that is of service to the built object. Space becomes "anti-space,"[1] and the ability of the building to define the public and private space is severely weakened. The modern notion of the "tower city"[2] has been under fire for the past several decades. The displeasure it has caused has provoked discussion of returning to the premodern notions of urban space as a solution to urban blight rather than, as Michael Dennis suggests, allowing both spatial configurations to exist—even at odds with each other—since they both contribute to the richness of the city.[3]

One of the results of this antimodern backlash is the rejection of the functionalist approach to urban design in favor of the conservationist approach. The functionalist attitude arose from the machine ethic of the Modern Movement, which was applied to the concepts of urban design. However, the conservationist approach is somewhat of a reaction to the blight sanctioned by urban renewal and its misuse of the functionalist attitude and the concepts of the Modern Movement.[4] As a result, we find those who would transform the concerns of the city into a political struggle.

The Neo-Rationalist outlook of Leon Krier takes on such a tone as he argues for the reconstruction of the city through the preservation and extension of the conceptual ordering of human values in the use of classical typological prescriptions for architecture. If used in the proper way with the European city type as a model, the city should achieve the coherence it lacks. Rob and Leon Krier both suggest this sort of prescriptive methodology for the problems of the architecture of the city. Rob Krier establishes a personal typology for the production of the urban environment based on a reductivist space "composed of squares, circles and triangles." His brother Leon utilizes invention and imagination in his visions of the city, an attitude springing from the Italian Rationalists such as Aldo Rossi, who sought not to use typology as convention or means of production but as a "mediating tool in the formal analysis of the city."[5]

The standards used today in many cities are based on European notions of good city form. These notions, however, do not take into consideration that which is of the United States. De Solà Morales refers to these methods, most commonly applied as the *mnemonic* approach, as a "recovery of certain figures of the city life of the past with the illusion that . . . in redeeming them, one [has] managed to recompose the lost civil attitude of the present-day city."[6] Such methods are based on premodern spatial concepts and are conservationist in character; whether prescriptive or performance-oriented in character, they tend to dictate a rationalist design philosophy. De Solà Morales sees this as opposite to the *rhetorical* approach, which is perhaps more relevant to the present condition in that it is "based on the direct portrayal of the new conditions specific to the modern city . . . removed from unity and linguistic redundancy, removed from abstract evocations and memory."[7]

Christopher Alexander, for example, formulates a theory of urban design based on a desire to heal the city through an architecture that is guided by growth toward wholeness.[8] While he does not go so far as to prescribe the necessary typology of design elements in his *A New Theory for Urban Design,* he does look nostalgically at the great cities of the past. He extracts rules of urbanism from them and applies them to today's cities, following the ONE rule, "Every increment of construction must be made in such a way as to heal the city . . . Every new act of construction has just one basic obligation; it must create a continuous structure of wholes around itself."[9] This desire to heal the city is, in essence, the reason for the existence of design guidelines in urban design policy today.

However, for the most part, the underlying thought behind this cure for what ails the contemporary city is a wholesale rejection of modernism in favor of a reaffirmation of the classical traditions. Alexander and his colleagues continue with "The Seven Detailed Rules of Growth," which read very much like a set of performance guidelines, rarely dictating solutions but certainly establishing an attitude toward urban design. This underlying foundation forms the basis upon which most prescriptive guidelines are developed. Having this in mind, let us examine the 12 cities to further demonstrate these ideas and consider other questions associated with the guidelines.

4.2 CASE STUDIES

Vail

As the years have passed, Vail has honed its design evaluation process so that the unique face of Vail is not truly alpine. In the introduction to revision of the Vail Village Urban Design Plan, the "Vail Village Design Considerations" (Figures 4.1 and 4.2), it states:

> Finally, it should be recognized that these guidelines *supplement* the Zoning Code but do not replace it. They are intended to influence the form and design of buildings. They do *not* establish maximum building floor areas, or land uses.[10]
> (Emphasis in the original)

Vail's *Zoning Title* paved a clear path for this approach in its discussion of design guidelines:

1. Structures shall be compatible with existing structures, their surroundings, and with Vail's environment. It is not to be inferred that buildings must look

alike to be compatible. Compatibility can be achieved through the proper consideration of scale, proportions, site planning, landscaping, materials and colors, and compliance with the guidelines herein contained.

2. Any building site in Vail is likely to have its own unique land forms and features. Whenever possible, these existing features should be preserved and reinforced by new construction. The objective is to fit the buildings to their sites in a way that leaves the natural land forms and features intact, treating the buildings as an integral part of the site, rather than as isolated objects at odds with their surroundings.[11]

Yet Vail's performance guidelines can become quite prescriptive. On roofs, for example:

Wood shakes, wood shingles, and built-up tow and gravel . . . [are] used almost exclusively for roofs in the Village. . . . For consistency, other roofing materials should be visually similar.[12]

On materials:

Stucco, brick, wood and glass are the primary building materials found in the Village. Within this small range of materials much variation and individuality are possible but too many diverse materials weaken the continuity of the streetscape.[13]

On color:

There is greater latitude in the use of color in the Village than in the use of materials, but there is still a discernible consistency within a general range of colors.
. . . Bright colors (such as red, orange, blue, maroon) should be avoided for major wall planes, but can be effective (used with restraint) for decorative trim, wall graphics, and other accent elements.[14]

Even in Vail, where there is strong desire for compatibility, there is room for creativity.

Vail's design guidelines for Vail Village and for Lionshead are manifestations of district focus. Additionally, there are design regulations for subareas, the commercial core of Vail Village, for example. Yet we also find that Vail has evidenced a concern for the entire town. Although we find that the town-wide regulations tend to be more general than those of Vail Village and Lionshead, landscaping has received special attention. Vail's Design Review Board has to exercise a great deal of discretion in determining the fit of a project with Vail's setting. Braun and Winston (1986) admit that subjective

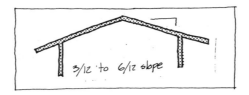

3/12 to 6/12 slope

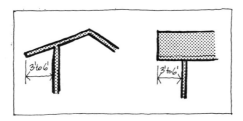

3' to 6'   3' to 6'

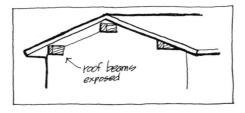

← roof beams
exposed

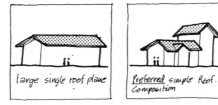

large single roof plane   Preferred simple Roof.
                                 Composition

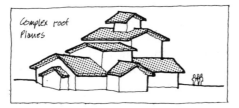

Complex roof
planes

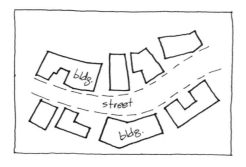

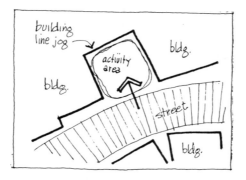

Figures 4.1 and 4.2. Examples of Vail design guidelines to create the "homey" look and feel, a total control of architectural concept. (*Source:* Vail Village Design Considerations, 1980, Vail, Colorado.)

criteria are harder to use than "standard zoning requirements." The result has been

> varying interpretation of what constitutes adequate compliance.... It is not uncommon for Planning [and Environmental] Commission decisions to be appealed to the Town Council over these interpretive matters.[15]

Just as Alexander, in his "Seven Detailed Rules of Growth," prescribes very little, yet establishes a framework and an attitude set forth through guidelines, Vail manifests its desired direction of growth through its guidelines.

Seattle

Seattle sets great store on livability and is very conscious of its image, but one might ask how the city sets about achieving ambience. The answer, again, is that the city is looking to the "magic" of guidelines to create this ambience (Figure 4.3). Success has come with (or perhaps in spite of) a project-by-project approach with city-wide evaluation by the design commission limited to city projects or projects on city land. Each project has its own standards or goals, developed in the evaluation process after the particular department proposing the project tells the design commission what the department has in mind.

A 1983 Progress Report from the design commission indicates their concern with consistency. The committee reports support for street tree plantings and "a policy against curb cuts . . . [and for] economy of maintenance."[16] We hardly need observe that design standards in historic districts are district focused and tend toward being prescriptive in nature. In the International Historic District there has been division into subareas with goal statements set for each of them. However, they often relate to maintaining the aura of the district's predominant era. In the International Historic District, there is emphasis on retaining the Oriental character of the existing buildings and continuing it in new construction. In other historic districts we observe very specific prescriptive standards on signage, facades, colors, textures, and siding materials.

We can find another facet of design evaluation by city staff of the Department of Construction and Land Use. Admittedly, the department has a code focus and responsibility; but as design concerns and issues have come to the fore, discretionary views of living up to the spirit of an ordinance have brought Seattle into conflict with some of its property owners, developers, and citizens over interpretations. Achieving some very general goals, such as avoiding high-density development and making housing available to all income groups, has necessitated some quite specific prescriptive standards such as FAR bonuses and TDRs.

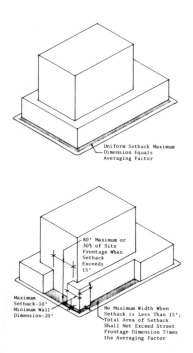

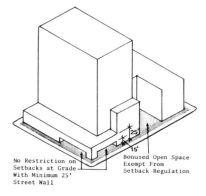

- Any exterior public open space in conformance with a public benefit feature described in Policy 23: Floor Area Bonus System, or provided to meet residential open space requirements shall be exempt from the calculation of the setback area permitted through the averaging technique.

- Where sidewalk widening is required to conform to the minimum width specified by Policy 8: Street Classification System, setback standards shall be referenced to the line established by the new sidewalk width.

EXCEPTIONS TO SETBACK REQUIREMENTS

Figure 4.3. Examples of design guidelines regarding setback requirements. (*Source:* Mayor's Recommended Land Use and Transportation Plan for Downtown Seattle, 1984, City of Seattle.)

San Francisco

San Francisco's Zoning Ordinance of 1985 is quite prescriptive in nature with its thorough delineation of many details of development in the C-3 District downtown. Included are particular areas and subareas for offices, retail, hotel/general, support commercial, and conservation. The urban design guidelines, a part of the zoning ordinance for the downtown area, tend to be performance-oriented in context, opting toward such concerns as human scale development and policies and principles of design criteria. Their focus is directed to districts of varying types. Preservation guidelines that discuss enhancing property values, maintaining a healthy economy, or keeping San Francisco attractive could be categorized as performance guidelines.

We hear so much about controlling growth and protecting ambience in downtown San Francisco that we might conclude wrongfully that there are no urban design evaluations city-wide. However, San Francisco's Master Plan includes an urban design section that dates back to 1971 (Figures 4.4 and 4.5).

URBAN DESIGN PRINCIPLES FOR STREET VIEWS AND SPACE

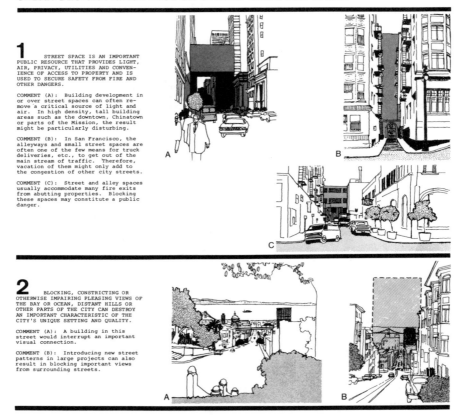

1   STREET SPACE IS AN IMPORTANT PUBLIC RESOURCE THAT PROVIDES LIGHT, AIR, PRIVACY, UTILITIES AND CONVENIENCE OF ACCESS TO PROPERTY AND IS USED TO SECURE SAFETY FROM FIRE AND OTHER DANGERS.

COMMENT (A):   Building development in or over street spaces can often remove a critical source of light and air. In high density, tall building areas such as the downtown, Chinatown or parts of the Mission, the result might be particularly disturbing.

COMMENT (B):   In San Francisco, the alleyways and small street spaces are often one of the few means for truck deliveries, etc., to get out of the main stream of traffic. Therefore, vacation of them might only add to the congestion of other city streets.

COMMENT (C):   Street and alley spaces usually accommodate many fire exits from abutting properties. Blocking these spaces may constitute a public danger.

2   BLOCKING, CONSTRICTING OR OTHERWISE IMPAIRING PLEASING VIEWS OF THE BAY OR OCEAN, DISTANT HILLS OR OTHER PARTS OF THE CITY CAN DESTROY AN IMPORTANT CHARACTERISTIC OF THE CITY'S UNIQUE SETTING AND QUALITY.

COMMENT (A):   A building in this street would interrupt an important visual connection.

COMMENT (B):   Introducing new street patterns in large projects can also result in blocking important views from surrounding streets.

Figure 4.4. Urban design principles for street views and space. (*Source:* San Francisco Urban Design Study Preliminary Report, 1970, City of San Francisco.)

Ahead of its time, the "Urban Design Plan" speaks of human needs and fundamental principles for city pattern, conservation, new development, and neighborhood environment. Policies to achieve these desirable "relationship[s] between people and their environment" included performance standards with illustrations in the plan to clarify their ideas.[17] The people of San Francisco still strongly embrace the idea of preserving neighborhood.

The "Bernal Heights East Slope Building Guidelines" state:

> The East Slope of Bernal Heights occupies a special place in the hearts of its residents. To those who would join us, we extend a cordial welcome and ask that they develop their properties and create their homes in such a way as to preserve

URBAN DESIGN PRINCIPLES FOR STREETS: INTERSECTIONS

1 THE TYPE AND LOCATION OF TRAFFIC CONTROL ELEMENTS AT AN INTERSECTION CAN VISUALLY REINFORCE THE FUNCTIONAL IMPORTANCE OF INTERSECTING STREETS.

COMMENT: This principle is tied quite closely to the amount of control these traffic signs provide. For instance, intersecting collector streets usually have only stop signs or yield signs. Arterial streets, of course, have the most control, with traffic signals and pedestrian crossing systems. Consistent use of control elements for each type of intersection is important.

2 THE QUANTITY OF INFORMATION DISPLAYED AT AN INTERSECTION INDICATES THE FUNCTIONAL IMPORTANCE OF THE STREET.

COMMENT: Residential streets have relatively little need to display information to a driver other than street names. Other types of street intersections should provide relatively more amounts of information, such as "one-way", "49 Mile Drive" or destination signs.

3 THE WIDTH OF INTERSECTING STREETS CAN VISUALLY REFLECT THEIR FUNCTIONAL IMPORTANCE.

COMMENT: Narrowing residential and collector streets and intersections would clearly indicate that they are less important. Such narrowing would also tend to decrease the volume and speed of traffic entering residential areas. In the Sunset District, where all streets are either 70 feet or 80 feet wide, regardless of their functional role as residential streets, application of this design principle would clarify their intended use. Major collectors, secondary streets, and major thoroughfares would not benefit from such a treatment.

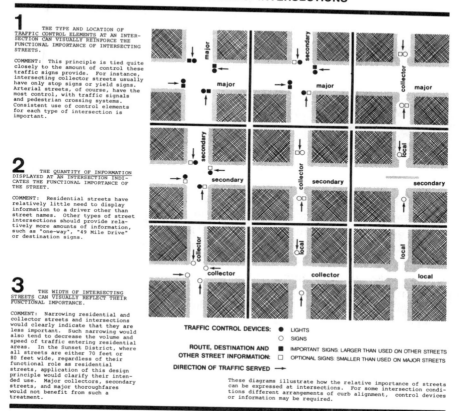

TRAFFIC CONTROL DEVICES: ● LIGHTS
○ SIGNS

ROUTE, DESTINATION AND
OTHER STREET INFORMATION: ■ IMPORTANT SIGNS: LARGER THAN USED ON OTHER STREETS
□ OPTIONAL SIGNS: SMALLER THAN USED ON MAJOR STREETS

DIRECTION OF TRAFFIC SERVED →

These diagrams illustrate how the relative importance of streets can be expressed at intersections. For some intersection conditions different arrangements of curb alignment, control devices or information may be required.

Figure 4.5. Urban design principles for street intersections. (*Source:* San Francisco Urban Design Study Preliminary Report, 1970, City of San Francisco.)

and enhance the qualities inherent to this special place. It is anticipated that these guidelines will encourage builders to design homes responsive to the unique character found on the East Slope.[18]

The East Slope Building Review Board's procedures call for evaluation of proposed development early in the architect's work so that the guidelines may impact plans and provide new projects that comingle with earlier development and the special environment of Bernal Heights. The guidelines are a mix of prescriptive and performance standards which reveal a sensitivity to the problem of rules stifling creativity.

Hence, while the discussion of choosing color and materials includes the idea that this is "a very personal decision of the future owner," there is a suggestion that a tour of the area would reveal any number of possible choices and a caution about the use of masonry veneers and plywood.[19] The "rules" on curb cuts and single garage doors are very prescriptive: garage doors no more than 10'0" wide, curb cut of 9'0" so positioned that there is 16'0" of curb space with a 25'0" wide lot, etc.[20] San Francisco clearly has found the adoption of both performance and prescriptive standards helpful in achieving urban design goals for the city.

San Diego

San Diego has developed plans for many different types of districts or areas with site-specific urban design guidelines for each. It all began in Centre City San Diego. Building on very detailed prescriptive standards in the zoning ordinances, the urban design guidelines in the original Centre City Plan (1976) were general performance guidelines. The 1983 "Urban Design Program, Centre City San Diego" is for the redevelopment project areas and applies to projects, "developed by means of a Disposition and Development Agreement (DDA), a Development Agreement (DA), or when a project encroaches on the public right of way."[21] The Centre City Development Commission expressed the hope that other developers would heed the program as well. After establishing the concepts, policies, and principles in general performance standards,

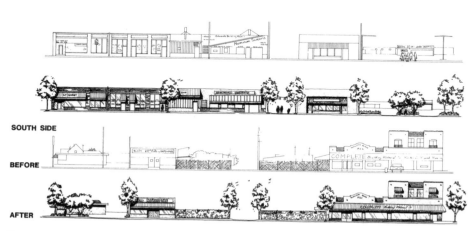

Figure 4.6. Design guidelines for University Avenue included in mid-city community plan, San Diego, California. An example of guidelines which emphasize cityscape versus classic preservationist model. (*Source:* Mid-City Design Plan, 1984, City of San Diego Planning Department.)

Part Two of the program, "Implementation and Standards," became quite specific and prescriptive, with detailed instructions for street lighting, paving, and landscaping.

We discover how San Diego has continued district focus and neighborhood participation in its City Ordinance 0-16921 (new series):

> The Southeast San Diego Community Planning Committee shall review discretionary permits in the manner established by Council Policy 600-24 which provides for community review of ongoing projects and plan implementation.[22]

Their advisory design evaluation efforts are in addition to those of the Southeast Economic Development Corporation's Board.

Specific prescriptive standards are set for "all public facilities, redevelopment projects, open spaces, streets, sidewalks, street furniture, street signs, lighting installations," etc.; and they must "conform to purpose and intent of this Division."[23] Thus, directives for evaluation exist to satisfy both general performance and specific prescriptive standards. It would appear, then, that in areas of redevelopment, historic interest, and special environmental problems (coastal resources zone, hillsides, flood hazard areas, etc.), San Diego has developed elaborate plans, ordinances, urban design guidelines, and environmental requirements (Figures 4.6, 4.7, and 4.8).

City urban design measures cover only landscaping, signage, and fences.

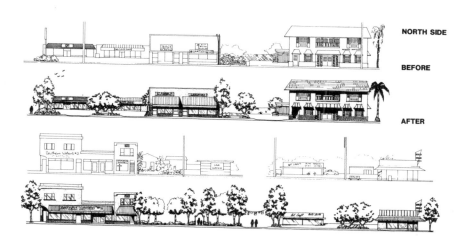

NORTH SIDE

BEFORE

AFTER

Guideline 4A—Site and design buildings to minimize pedestrian/vehicle conflicts.

Example: Avoid locating driveways, garage ramps or loading and service areas where they interfere with the flow of pedestrian movement or impact the activities of pedestrian space.

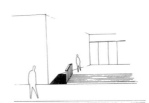

Guideline 4B—The design of pedestrian spaces should consider the special needs of the handicapped.

Example: Sidewalks, street furnishings, roadside curbs, pedestrian ramps, etc. should be designed to allow safe and efficient use of pedestrian spaces by handicapped persons.

Guideline 4C—Site buildings to create new pedestrian spaces that complement the use of the Existing Pedestrian Rights-of-way.

Example: Buildings are set back to create plazas and allow wider sidewalks along an important pedestrian street.

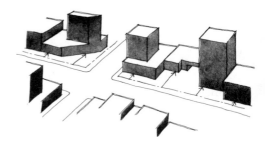

Figures 4.7. and 4.8. Examples of design guidelines included in the City of San Diego urban design program regarding relationship of building and street not based on traditional city model. (*Source:* Urban design program, Centre City San Diego, 1983, by Centre City Development Corporation.)

Additionally, in areas with slopes of more than 25 percent and a minimum elevation of 50 feet, the Hillside Review Overlay Zone applies. The Resource Protection Overlay Zone ordinance provides some protection of the environment in areas in which it is presently deemed necessary. These measures blend performance guides and detailed prescriptive standards.

Portland

Portland seems to have felt comfortable with establishing broad goals, again first for the downtown area. Here, performance standards have allowed great leeway in application by the design commission, which looks for creative solutions to problems that will result ultimately in enhancing the existing character, promoting diversity and areas of special character, providing a rich

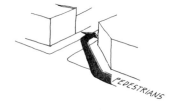

Example: Building setbacks can be used to facilitate movements around corners where large numbers of pedestrians are expected to circulate. This technique can also be used to encourage pedestrians to follow desired pathways.

Guideline 4D—Site and design structures to facilitate public access across sites where important pedestrian movements occur.

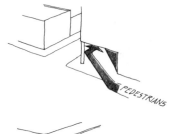

Example: Lower level pathways can be used where building setbacks are not possible.

Example: Mid-block passageways can be created to allow pedestrian circulation through a fully developed site. Passageways that are open rather than covered relate better to pedestrian street activity.

and diverse pedestrian experience, and humanizing the downtown. The guidelines for carrying out these goals continue a performance orientation.

Portland has responded to the needs of special districts with carefully drawn guidelines. Gaudy signage is part of Broadway's appeal, and a different type of signage is permitted in Chinatown. Guidelines for development of the South Waterfront Area speak in general performance terms about the direction of the development: emphasizing pedestrian ways to link this area with other areas; permitting buildings with a common theme but diverse types; encouraging consistent landscaping throughout, etc. The main thrust is toward strengthening ties to the Willamette River. As in other cities, guidelines in historic districts get quite specific—prescriptive standards in action.

With all this varied experience behind them, Portland's Planning Department was able to frame a solid document in January 1988, *Recommended Central City Plan*. Policy 12, "Urban Design", is general where it can be general and specific where prescriptive guidelines are needed (Figures 4.9 and 4.10). Therefore, we find a repetition of previous calls for protection of view corridors, followed by a recommendation that the "Central City FAR and Building Height's Map" be adopted with the plan. This is a performance

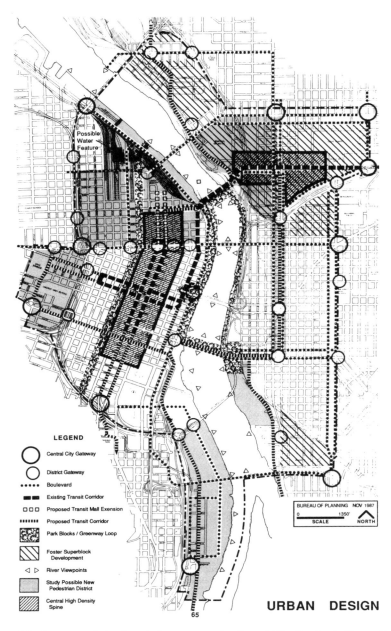

LEGEND

○ Central City Gateway

○ District Gateway

••••• Boulevard

▬ ▬ Existing Transit Corridor

□□□ Proposed Transit Mall Extension

▪▪▪▪▪▪ Proposed Transit Corridor

Park Blocks / Greenway Loop

Foster Superblock Development

◁ ▷ River Viewpoints

Study Possible New Pedestrian District

Central High Density Spine

BUREAU OF PLANNING   NOV 1987

0 _____ 1350'
SCALE   NORTH

URBAN   DESIGN

Figure 4.9. Recommended urban design concept for Central City Portland. (*Source:* Recommended Central City Plan, 1988, Portland Bureau of Planning.)

Enhance the Central City as a livable, walkable area which focuses on the river and captures the glitter and excitement of city living.

FURTHER:

A. Create a rich and enjoyable environment for pedestrians throughout the Central City.

B. Strive for excellence in the design of new buildings.

C. Encourage designers of new developments to sensitively enhance Portland's human scale of buildings, streets and open spaces.

D. Promote the formation of districts with distinct character and a diverse and rich mixture of uses (in nonindustrial areas).

E. Identify and protect significant public views.

F. Locate the highest densities in the Downtown and along potential and existing transit corridors, and step density down toward the Willamette River, residential neighborhoods adjacent to the Central City, and as the distance from the core increases.

Figure 4.10. A classic example of urban design recommendations for Central City Portland. (*Source:* Recommended Central City Plan, 1988, Portland Bureau of Planning.)

measure followed by prescriptive standards to achieve it. The recommended zoning code amendments will further tighten prescriptive measures to meet the broad goals of the document. Portland is still at work on an update of the zoning code to "include restructuring the City's commercial zones and mapping the zoning boundaries and designations to reflect the new zones."[24]

Minneapolis

While Minneapolis may lack in guidelines to continue to influence desired urban design goals for development projects, the Committee on the Urban Environment (CUE) steps in to fill the breech. The reader will recall that efforts to expand and formalize urban design evaluation were defeated in 1983. CUE has remained active in promoting performance standards, good urban design, and citizen participation. While the city does not evaluate all development, CUE again will make recommendations for improving all projects. The focus of design evaluation is city-wide, with district emphasis only in the downtown and historic districts.

Minneapolis's planning efforts have maintained a long-range perspective.

Thirty years ago Minneapolis began anticipating the year 2000, asking what directions the city should take to reach its goals. In January 1988, the City Planning Department issued the latest update, "Metro 2000 Plan: Minneapolis Metro Center." All these goal-setting efforts have been joint city and private ventures. This was perhaps done to assure greater adherence to the established performance standards.

Lincoln

While Lincoln has had carefully formulated urban design guidelines since 1981, only city projects or private projects on public property are subject to design evaluation. Let us quickly add an exception to that seemingly definitive statement: Also subject to evaluation by the Lincoln Urban Design Committee is the construction of buildings, distribution substations, and ground-level switching stations by public and private utility companies, *and* construction in historic districts or within 300 feet of a designated historic landmark unless the Historic Preservation Commission has evaluated the project.

Lincoln's urban design guidelines present a performance orientation while they are quite flexible. The committee wants to see a site plan (with inclusion of some items specified) and to hear about any possible adverse effects and how they may be ameliorated. Their concerns are general: "To further the attractiveness of Lincoln as a place to live and work, . . . [to] enhance public and private investment, . . . to encourage improved quality and functional utility of development. . . ."[25]

The city has set careful limits on aspects to be evaluated. The evaluation is "to promote a desirable man-made urban environment and . . . to protect natural physical features, . . . to encourage the harmonious use of color, texture and materials," etc.[26] The most specific of the directives:

> To assure that reasonable consideration has been given to . . . the need for sound and sight buffers, the preservation of views and solar access and other aspects of design which may have significant impact upon the urban design fabric of the community.

The restrictions on committee activity are quite stringent: They are to provide guidance but may not "design or assist in design," they must keep costs of their suggestions in mind, and they "shall not review detailed technical or engineering aspects of review items."[27]

Although Lincoln has had urban design evaluation in place since 1981, it almost appears as if the concerns for interference with private development and the territories of the zoning ordinances and historic preservation would tend to make their urban design evaluation approach of limited effectiveness. It remains to be seen whether this is truly the case.

Kansas City

In contrast to the situation in Lincoln, Kansas City has an extensive set of urban design guidelines with wide application. The four sections of the "Kansas City Urban Design Guidebook" address neighborhoods, major streets and centers, landscape, and buildings. The concern is city-wide, with neighborhoods (districts) receiving special protection. Since the city has been divided into 46 planning areas, it is these areas individually, rather than the entire city, that tend to get attention. Kansas City and its Redevelopment Authority both depend on performance-oriented guidelines, leaving design details to the architect. The evaluation process itself leads the architect to follow the broad directives of the urban design policy (Figures 4.11 and 4.12).

Irvine

Irvine's urban design guidelines have to be highly prescriptive to guarantee the uniformity of design within communities and subareas which The Irvine Company demands and to which the city acquiesces. The architects have more creative leeway in the industrial and commercial areas. Here the guidelines are more performance oriented with emphasis on environmental concerns rather than on design conformance. Design evaluation in Irvine is city-wide within a framework provided by the zoning ordinances. Overlay, Environmental and the Civic District Overlay Districts maintain district-level guidelines which narrow the development possibilities and are a bit more prescriptive in their focus.

Indianapolis

Indianapolis has 28 separate districts that are recognized in the 1981 Regional Center General Plan. It is the particular nature of each of these districts that sets the focus of design evaluation in each of them. There are no written guidelines, but the planning staff looks at the techniques used for the management and enhancement of urban design elements. In the case of the Regional Center Plan, the identified elements included land use, building style, color, texture, proportion, rhythm, scope and degree of maintenance, amount of open space, light, air, etc. (Figure 4.13). This smacks of performance evaluation. The Central Business District has development standards set in the zoning code. As in the other districts and subareas, both prescriptive and performance standards are in place. The innovative "sky exposure plane" has definitive prescriptive standards. The net result is that Indianapolis enforces only those standards set in the zoning ordinances and relies on the evaluation process to try to exert influence on architects and developers to consider what the city wants.

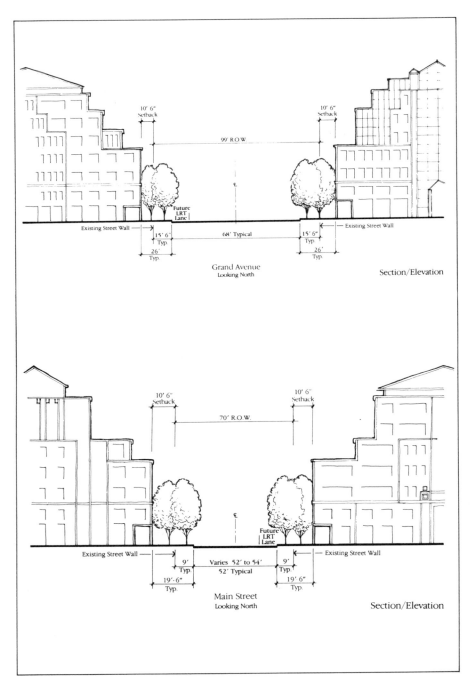

Figure 4.11. Kansas City proposed design guidelines for street cross sections based on classical notions of grand boulevards. (*Source:* Grand/Main Corridor Study 1987/HNTB.)

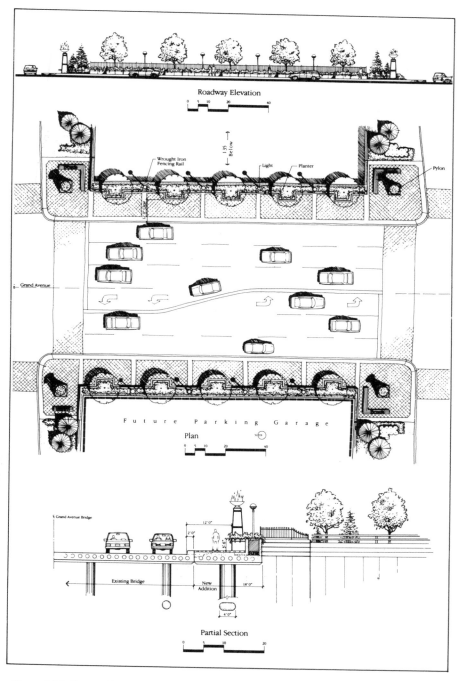

Roadway Elevation

Wrought Iron Fencing Rail

I-35 Below

Light

Planter

Pylon

Grand Avenue

Future Parking Garage

Plan

Grand Avenue Bridge

12' 0"

2' 0"

Existing Bridge

New Addition

18' 0"

4' 0"

Partial Section

Figure 4.12. Kansas City proposed design guidelines for Grand Avenue and Main Street Bridge at I-35, an example of a return of the city to its past. (*Source:* Grand/Main Corridor Study 1987, HNTB.)

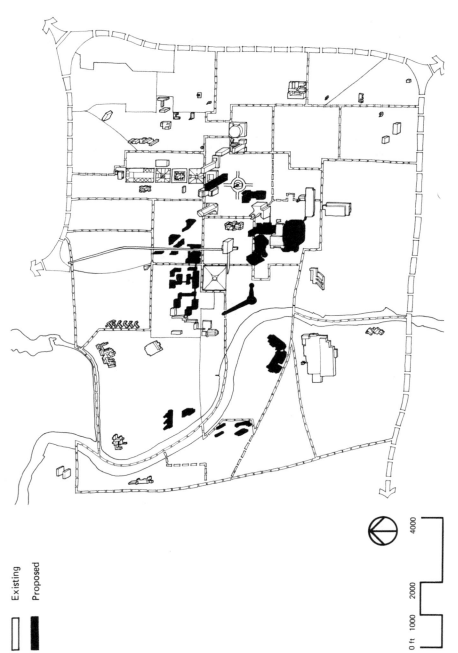

Figure 4.13. Architectural structure of Indianapolis with landmarks representing a layer in the history of city development. (*Source:* Indianapolis 1980–2000, Regional Center General Plan, 1981, Division of Planning and Zoning, City of Indianapolis.)

Existing

Proposed

0 ft 1000   2000   4000

Dallas

Not all development is subject to design evaluation in Dallas. Therefore, the city relies heavily on the detailed and prescriptive standards of zoning ordinances to influence the architecture of the city. City-wide design evaluation covers only landscaping, signage, and planned development districts. The requirements for landscaping and signage are very specific, detailed, and prescriptive: Use these landscape materials, screen off-street loading areas this way, use one or more trees in landscaping, erect no billboards in nonbusiness districts, signs attached to a building must be flat, signs on a single-family or duplex house can only be for-sale signs, etc. (Figures 4.14 and 4.15).

In the planned districts, a Design Standards Test determines the points a proposed project will receive for paying proper attention to building color, facade material, streetscape improvements, awnings and arcades, retail-related usages, parking lot screening, etc. The planning director also may consult with district or neighborhood committees to ascertain their concerns. The four officially recognized districts—Oak Lawn and State-Thomas Special Purpose, Dallas Arts and Near Eastside Development—have been encouraging urban design.

Baltimore

Baltimore's Historic Preservation Guidelines apply city-wide. The requirements for new construction or renovation are found in very restrictive prescriptive guidelines, even to the point of specifying particular features of eighteenth and early, mid-, or late nineteenth century buildings. There are directions for the most commonly repaired or replaced architectural elements: windows and doors, porches and steps, stairways, fire escapes, roofs, architectural metals, walls, fences and railings, and commercial signs. Of necessity, approval by the Commission for Historical and Architectural Preservation (CHAP) has to be discretionary, at least in part. The commission members will examine plans for new development and for repair to see if these plans adequately conform to specifications or create the illusion of conforming.

With Baltimore's predilection for recognizing neighborhoods, it should be no surprise that design evaluation generally has a neighborhood or project orientation. In the Inner Harbor Area Redevelopment Plan are 26 development areas, some further divided into subareas. Special prescriptive regulations apply in each area so that each of them may fulfill a particular function: public, residential, commercial-residential, commercial, or semipublic. In the evaluation process, the board will look at specific prescriptive items but keep the overall performance goals in mind: ". . . Establish and maintain values and insure aesthetic and functional coordination to carrying out the objectives of the Renewal Plan and the continued maintenance of the Project."[28]

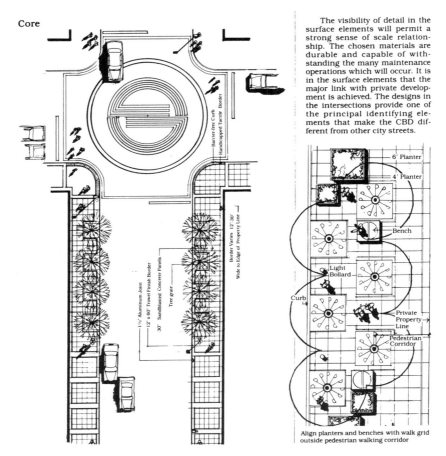

Core

The visibility of detail in the surface elements will permit a strong sense of scale relationship. The chosen materials are durable and capable of withstanding the many maintenance operations which will occur. It is in the surface elements that the major link with private development is achieved. The designs in the intersections provide one of the principal identifying elements that make the CBD different from other city streets.

6' Planter
4' Planter
Bench
Light Bollard
Curb
Private Property Line
Pedestrian Corridor
Align planters and benches with walk grid outside pedestrian walking corridor

Figures 4.14. and 4.15. Proposed Dallas Central Business District Streetscape Guidelines, an example of beautification of the city. (*Source:* Dallas Center Business District Streetscape, n.d., Myrick, Newman, Dahlberg Inc.)

Input from the Design Advisory Panel (DAP) or CHAP or by a special evaluation board in a redevelopment project tempered by the recommendations of neighborhood groups may be necessary steps in the evaluation of a project. One of the problems associated with Baltimore's evaluation process is the likelihood of an abrupt change in design from one project to another. A different neighborhood brings a different set of values to bear. The existence of several special districts also dampens the neighborhood approach to design evaluation. Regardless of the neighborhood, if a project is in a Flood Hazard or Critical Areas zone, a redevelopment area, or a parking or historic district, special prescriptive guidelines are applicable in addition to any neighborhood concerns.

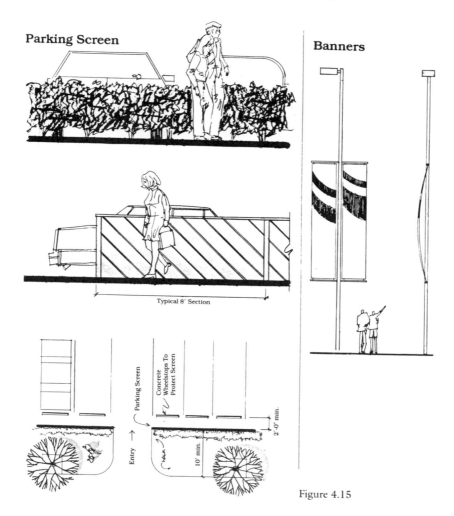

Figure 4.15

4.3 THE COMMON GROUND

By examining the above cases, we can draw several conclusions. First, in general, the overall categories of performance and prescriptive guidelines are reasonably correct. In particular, performance guidelines can be rationalized based on quantifiable, objective standards concerned with public health and safety as well as adverse environmental impact. However, one important problem associated with performance guidelines in many cities studied here is that many guidelines identified by the cities as "performance" are not or cannot be categorized as such, due in part to the basically prescriptive nature of their premise. The other main problem is that performance guidelines are restricted to relatively few items in the evaluation process and are not applied to a variety of interrelated elements.

For example, the whole notion of building envelope, which deals with light, shadow, view, and solar energy as well as other issues of building environment, should also be linked to exterior concerns such as parking, traffic volume, sewage and disposal capacity, water supply, and many other aspects of urban physical development. These are logical categories for the application of performance evaluation, and they are necessary if we are to protect public health, safety, and welfare. It is vital for the city to relate performance guidelines to urban and regional infrastructure systems, lest they be treated only in a superficial, fragmented manner; the result will certainly not be responsive enough to produce a functional city of quality. The performance guidelines have a built-in flexibility that responds to the architect's inclination toward invention and creativity rather than an assembly of prescribed formal vocabulary.

The prescriptive guidelines, on the other hand, are based on many assumptions that can be questioned because of their predetermined notions of what the architecture of the city should be. By closely examining these 12 cities, one can make two observations. First, many of these guidelines are very generic, and therefore subject to interpretation. In application, such guidelines are basically used as political ammunition for the discretionary evaluation process; that is to say, the evaluation body has free rein in spite of the portrayed objectivity of the evaluation process.

Second, when and if the guidelines are more specific and perhaps at times even too focused, they are essentially duplicated from district to district and city to city, used as prototypes of "good" environments. This tendency is creating what I have referred to elsewhere as franchised packages of codified design elements, heavily based on economic and marketing issues rather than on architecture of the city.[29] We will be examining many of these examples in the next chapter, but the fundamental issue here is that these guidelines are protecting or promoting economic development based on short-term benefits and not the long-term public institution.

REFERENCE NOTES

1. Steven K. Peterson, "Space and Anti-Space," *Harvard Architecture Review* 1 (Spring 1980):89ff.
2. Michael Dennis, *Court and Garden* (Cambridge, MA: MIT Press, 1986), 216.
3. Ibid., 216–217.
4. David Gosling and Barry Maitland, *Concepts of Urban Design* (New York: St. Martin's Press, 1984).
5. Micha Bandini, "Typology as a Form of Convention," *AA Files* 6 (May 1984):77–80.

6. Ignasi de Solà Morales, "Mnemosis or Rhetoric: The Crisis of Representation in Modern City and Architecture," in *Beyond the City, The Metropolis,* ed. Georges Teyssot (Milan: Electa, 1988), 177.

7. Ibid.

8. Hamid Shirvani, "Context as Coherence in Discourse," *Urban Design and Preservation Quarterly* 12, No. 1/2 (1989):37.

9. Christopher Alexander et al., *A New Theory of Urban Design* (New York: Oxford University Press, 1987), 22.

10. Winston Associates, "Preliminary Draft of Vail Village [CO] Design Considerations," July 30, 1986, 3.

11. Town of Vail, *Zoning Title,* 18.54.050, 1983, 54.

12. Winston Associates, "Preliminary Draft of Vail Village [CO] Design Considerations," July, 30, 1986, 15.

13. Ibid., 17.

14. Ibid.

15. Thomas A. Braun and Jeffrey T. Winston, "The Vail Village Urban Design Guide Plan: A Framework for Guiding Development," *UD Review* 9, No. 4 (Fall 1986):18.

16. City of Seattle, Department of Community Development, "Seattle Design Commission Progress Report," 1983, 2.

17. City of San Francisco, City Planning Commission, "Urban Design Plan," August 26, 1971, 1.

18. City of San Francisco, City Planning Commission and Bernal Heights Community Foundation, "Bernal Heights East Slope Building Guidelines," November 13, 1986, 1.

19. Ibid., 30.

20. Ibid., 31.

21. City of San Diego, Centre City Development Corporation (CCDC), "Urban Design Program, Centre City San Diego, Amendment," October 25, 1983, frontispiece.

22. City of San Diego, "Southeast San Diego Planned District," Ordinance 0-16921 (new series), Section 101.1702.C.4, August 3, 1987, 4.

23. Ibid., D,4.

24. City of Portland, "Amendments to Recommended Central City Plan," March 1988, 30.

25. City of Lincoln, *Zoning Ordinances,* Chapter 14.90.010, December 15, 1982, 532-13.

26. City of Lincoln, Urban Design Committee, "Bylaws," July 1, 1981, 4.

27. Ibid.

28. City of Baltimore, Department of Housing and Community Development, "Inner Harbor Project I Renewal Plan," originally approved June 15, 1967, and amended through May 8, 1985, 10.

29. Hamid Shirvani, "Architecture Versus Franchised Design," *Urban Design and Preservation Quarterly* 11, No. 2/3 (1988).

Chapter 5

SUBSTANTIVE ELEMENTS

All of our previous discussions of public evaluation of architecture of the city, the evaluation categories, the processes, the actors, and the context have finally brought us to the essence of the evaluation, "substantive elements." What is it that we are evaluating? Or, to put it another way, what is the content of evaluation? Given the current situation, how is the scope of architecture of the city determined within the evaluation process? And, finally, what are the premises of this defined architecture?

The common practice has been to divide the architectural and design substance into a variety of elements. These elements range from land use and building form to lighting fixtures and benches on the street. The key reason behind this categorization of content of architecture of the city has been the notion of classification and codification of design guidelines for the purpose of communication. In addition, categorization makes the process more objective and, perhaps, rationalized through various descriptive details. Yet another motive certainly is to associate these elements more closely with city zoning and land-use ordinances.

To begin, I reject this notion of categorization and codification and argue against this approach as one of the fundamental problems associated with the present practice of public architecture. I must, however, admit that elsewhere I have fallen into the same trap and have succumbed to the dangers of dealing with the issues of urban architecture in terms of black and white, using these categorizations in defining the scope of architecture of the city.[1] I will discuss my reasons for rejecting this notion at the end of this chapter. Moreover, since almost all of the cities we have examined in this book have somehow used this approach, I have had no other choice but to follow the same path in order to examine these categories closely and identify specific problems associated with them. As a result, I have assembled the cities' substantive elements into five general groups: land use, building form, circulation and parking, the landscape, and signage.

5.1 LAND USE

There is certainly an evolutionary history behind land-use planning. It has been and will continue to be one of the most fundamental structural forces in the American city. Land-use policy forms the basis for zoning ordinances and, thus, is directly responsible for a great deal of the architecture of the city as it has existed in the past. Land-use planning, therefore, is not simply a functional element of a hierarchial organization of land uses from industry down to residential and open space. Rather, it forms the underlying structural foundation and, together with building form, determines the physical framework for the architecture of the city. While the urban fabric has been largely determined or heavily influenced by land-use policies, the land-use plans and the resulting decisions are based on economic and political factors exclusive of any architectural input.

Accepting this norm as part of a market economy, land-use policy together with its sister element, building form, has to deal with a culture of fragments, architecture *within* versus architecture *of* the city. The culture of democratic marketing has already laid the ground, the structure, the context within which fragments of the architecture of the city evolve. The openness of the American city is an expression of freedom and democracy. The mechanism of this freedom is the grid, which as the primary divider of land has come to stand for the ownership and franchisement of the members of the democratic society.[2] Further "it liberates the city from the fetters of static social order and certainly expresses opportunity." These are not the qualities of the traditional city, the closed city, which relies less on architectural quality than it does on architectural compatibility.[3]

Interestingly enough, however, the specific design guidelines in regard to elements such as land use, building form, landscaping, and parking attempt to deal with a holistic notion of the city and with a melding of the fragments. The guidelines attempt to bring back the old city, the city of the past, the city as a whole, the 24-hour downtown, the mixed-use city core; meanwhile, the underlying structure is based on the fragmenting of market and democracy. An examination of our 12 cities reveals this point quite well. As we will see, either most cities are preoccupied with elementary notions of land use based on economic impact on both the public and the landowner, attempting to balance the two; *or* they have departed from the basics and are attempting to revive the city of the past.

San Francisco

San Francisco attempts to control development downtown, restricting density and building development in the direction of the city goals. However, there is much more to San Francisco's land-use plan. One important element is the separation of working areas from the residential areas. The city has planned that commercial and industrial development will be confined to the eastern part of the city from the bay to the inland hills. Here we find the downtown, business and services, and light and general industry areas. There are 12 residential areas, carefully separated by topographic or established boundaries and, in some cases, by traffic ways or open space. San Francisco has given thought to 24-hour usage downtown with office, shopping, financial, entertainment, apartment, and hotel development. The city rewards its developers with higher density allowances for provision of amenities. Many other cities also have used FARs, TDRs, and point systems to gain open space, view corridors, pedestrian ways, selectively reduced densities, public art, retailing, and other amenities. But, again, care in provision must be used. There is no reward in empty plazas, unused pedestrian ways, and poorly planned shopping areas.

Lincoln

The best move that Lincoln has made in its application of land-use policy is its cooperation with Lancaster County in a comprehensive plan. Some of the actions taken by the Planning Commission (March 27, 1988) reveal the status of zoning/land use in Lincoln. One example is the application for a permit for day care facilities in a single-family residential zone. In another case, a church in an R-6 residential zone with commercial on the south and suburban offices to the east and across the street wanted to increase its land use. Grandfathered with an existing coverage of 26.1 percent in a zone that permits a 15 percent lot coverage for churches, the church wanted to build a 20' × 20' storage building that would increase lot coverage to 27.1 percent. Because no suitable adjacent land was available, and because parking areas were not affected, the planning staff assigned but minimal impact to the request and recommended approval.

Of particular interest to our land-use discussion is a request to change a zone from R-4 Residential to I-2 Industrial. The applicant wanted to build a barn for storage of materials and equipment. The planning staff recommended a change of enough of the zone to allow for the barn since the land previously had been zoned industrial. The staff members attached a strong suggestion that an older residential area be retained as is and that industrial uses not encroach further.

Seattle

Seattle has land-use policies for the downtown, neighborhood commercial, single- and multifamily residential, open space (not yet accepted), industrial, and major institution areas. This is as it should be, for the zoning ordinances determine the finer points and set the limits for the land-use policies. The Seattle Downtown Plan has been in place since 1984. "The Land Use Policies define Downtown's functional areas and identify the general categories of use to be permitted, prohibited, or allowed under special conditions."[4] Seattle is interested in controlling the density of uses and the features of the natural and built environments. Therefore, there are 11 specified zones ranging from Downtown Office Core, to Downtown Harbor Front, to several historical districts, to an International District Residential. There is a clear concern for the retention of the waterfront amenities; by regulating future uses the city hopes to blur divisions between districts by encouraging similar usages.

Portland

Portland has been planning its land uses so that the north/south avenue pattern and appropriate view corridors following the course of the Willamette River have remained. Growth has brought development beyond the city lines into Multnomah and Washington counties. City zoning ordinances control land uses with Z zone regulations and design guidelines in the downtown. There also are recognized special districts. Information on land uses in Central City is up-to-date; the bureau of planning prepared a new "Predominant Land Use Map" in January 1988 based on 1985 information with some limited updating as part of a "Recommended Central City Plan." This map shows how complex development in Portland has become. What shows on the map as an office building, the predominant use, actually also may include retailing and below-grade parking.[5] Land uses outside Central City have not been catalogued since 1975, although the bureau of planning checked uses along the borders of Central City if those uses might be an issue within Central City.

Minneapolis ·

In Minneapolis the land-use categories include retailing, office, hotel, entertainment, housing, cultural, institutional, fringe and short-term parking ramps, and auto service usages. The city's "Metro 2000 Plan" charts the direction Minneapolis plans to take in the future. For example, downtown Minneapolis is the shopping center for a large area. It makes sense, therefore, to emphasize retailing with a focus on the Nicolet Mall area. One can anticipate what other urban design elements will receive attention because of this continuing retail development.

Yet, 80 percent of the jobs downtown are in offices; Minneapolis cannot ignore the importance of office land use. The "Metro 2000 Plan" anticipates a growth in office space of 770,000 square feet a year.[6] Minneapolis plans on continuing growth in many areas. We shall mention but one more, the convention emphasis area. New hotels will add 2300 more rooms for visitors. The entertainment district also supports tourism and conventions with expanded restaurants and the new Hennepin Center. Minneapolis is devoting a great deal of attention to land uses in its Metro Center in order to keep it livable and lively.

Kansas City

Recently, Kansas City has deliberately set about gentrification as a land-use policy in a specific downtown area, the Country Club Plaza, with the following official statement:

> The potential of the Plaza area as a location for luxury housing to complement the office development is also a great competitive advantage for Kansas City. While no city should make land-use policies solely for the most privileged members of its society, the commitment of high-income wage earners to reside within the City is important . . . because such people make location decisions about businesses and are likely to consider their own convenience in making these decisions.[7]

Let us hasten to add, however, that the plaza study also addressed the retention of existing neighborhoods to provide diverse housing opportunities. The City Development Department also commissioned a study that found "adequate relocation housing is available in good condition and with comparable rents."[8]

Kansas City squarely faced the issue of competition with its suburbs by undertaking the Plaza Plan. In order to remain competitive, this area's land use is providing for retaining its regional shopping center and high-rise office centers with appropriate housing and services. Within redevelopment areas, a project-by-project approach might tend to determine general land-use policy. It is not that the redevelopment authority does not deal with land usages. They are quite concerned with densities and definition of land usages and their mix. And, of course, they must perform within the zoning ordinances. A constant watch would keep the land usages consistent and within desired limits.

Let us not overplay the possibility of lack of coordination of land-use planning. The Plaza Plan came into being because the city recognized that city plans prior to 1982 had not anticipated the pressures of growth in the Country Club Plaza area. When the city saw this as a problem, it began planning and urban design recommendations to guide development. Recall also that the city began a city-wide plan revision in 1987.[9]

Irvine

Irvine's preoccupation with a unified city image dictates close attention to a land-use policy/plan. Indeed, the first 22 pages of the "City of Irvine General Plan" deal with land issues.[10] Such a plan is essential for the precise phasing of development within Irvine's prescribed areas. Irvine has planned for the following land uses:

1. Residential villages
2. "A regional commercial center"
3. "Major businesses and industrial complexes . . . along the eastern and western edges of the City"
4. Agricultural area near El Toro, the Marine Corps Air Station
5. "Very low density residential development in the rugged, more environmentally sensitive foothill areas"
6. University of California (Irvine)
7. An "east-west activity corridor"
8. "North-south open space corridors"

Defined as key determinant of land-use policy is that

> the Land Use Element does not contain a final picture of the City in the future, but an expression of what is desired for the future based on present knowledge and circumstances, and as such, is part of a continuous planning process.[11]

Indianapolis

As in Lincoln, Indianapolis's joint efforts with Marion County have enabled, both entities to structure development to their mutual interest. Thus we find plans for a Regional Center and a joint City-County Council of 29 members. The Department of Metropolitan Development oversees the Unigov area, which formerly had 17 different planning areas. Downtown revitalization has poured more than a billion dollars in public and private funds into thoughtfully planned development.

The design guidelines for the Regional Center were being developed in 1988. Land use probably will not receive as much attention as the other design elements in the guidelines because the "Indianapolis 1980–2000: Regional Center General Plan" sets forth proposed changes in land use.[12] Existing land uses in the Regional Center area (5.4 square miles in size) include public and semipublic, commercial, residential, industrial, parks and open space, mixed-use, parking, vacant, and streets right of way. The plan anticipates that there will be a "dramatic decrease in vacant and industrial land

and parking." Countering this will be a "significant increase in parks and open space, public and semi-public land," and residential usage in the downtown.[13]

Dallas

Dallas is working on a new zoning ordinance which will satisfy the policies established in an earlier planning policy. This new zoning, along with Dallas's basic land-use plan, enables the city to better manage its land resource. Apparently there have been problems with incompatible uses and conflicting densities. Therefore, the new code will attempt restrictions on certain usages in close proximity to specified existing uses such as single-family housing.

Dallas's core area developed rapidly in the period 1966-1988, with an increase of high-rise office buildings from 7 to 16. In the so-called Frame Area of 700 acres around the Core, there have been great changes as well. An aerial photograph shows parking areas continue as "a conspicuous land use."[14] Ponte and Travers do not feel that the Core area will expand much farther; it grew from 150 to 200 acres between 1968 and 1986. They observe:

> Two hundred acres is the average size for Core areas in North American cities, a fact due to the need for enterprises located in the Core to be in close proximity to each other. Once that limit has been reached, variations in land coverage are minimal. Further growth tends to be upwards into taller and taller buildings.[15]

Baltimore

It should be no surprise that Baltimore, the city of neighborhoods, last revised its city-wide zoning 20 years ago. This partly explains the previously mentioned difficulty of one neighborhood's land use conflicting with an abutting neighborhood's land use. Within organized neighborhoods and special districts (historic, flood hazard, critical areas, parking, and urban renewal), land uses are clearly specified.

Baltimore emphasizes mixing usages to provide 24-hour activity in the neighborhoods, districts, and redevelopment areas. An example is the permitted land uses in Inner Harbor Project I Renewal Plan. General permitted uses include commercial, residential, commercial residential, semipublic, public, marine storage, and fabrication and industrial. Three to five specific uses, including parking, are permitted under each general use except industrial. That use is governed by zoning classification M-3, with some exceptions. Retail or ancillary retail uses are permitted in all except marine storage and fabrication and industrial zones. Certain uses are prohibited, and there are standards and controls which set maximum and minimum sizes for facilities and many other dos and don'ts on the two and one-half legal size pages.

Vail

In one sense, we might say that land-use characteristics in Vail have been predetermined by the nature of the terrain and by the presence of the I-70 corridor. But, on the other hand, Vail has been very deliberate in its efforts to determine its land uses. Therefore, we find the most intense land uses in and near Vail Village and Lionshead and a concern for the preservation of open space essential to the aura of Vail and to its primary industry, ski tourism. Mixed uses predominate in the core of Vail Village, and the emphasis is the fostering of 24-hour pedestrian activity. For more than ten years, Vail had no land-use controls; development proceeded unchecked, establishing the framework of present-day Vail. Now, however, Vail residents are sold on preservation and land-use controls. Flexible limitations on both retail and residential uses are tied to the Design Considerations Criteria of the proposed Vail Village Master Plan with an eye to encouraging suitable retail and short-term residential facilities.

San Diego

To examine land use in San Diego, we have to consider the basic zoning ordinance provisions and any district or overlay zones that apply. The "Urban Design Program, Centre City San Diego" in one of its policies speaks of creating "a mixed-use environment in Centre City by promoting residential, office, commercial, and institutional development."[16] Ordinance 0-16921 (new series), adopted on August 3, 1987, reveals that the city felt it was necessary to be *very* specific about land uses in the Southeast San Diego Planned District. The ordinance is described as *"reasonable* development criteria for the construction or alteration of *quality* residential, commercial and industrial development"[17] (author's emphasis). Throughout the ordinance we find references to premises not being used except for one or more uses as specified in Appendix A.

In Appendix A are 11 pages of "permitted uses," but the lines are drawn even finer. The Southeast San Diego Planned District has residential zones (SF and MF), commercial categories (1, 2, and 3) , and Industrial Zones (I-1 and I-2). Therefore, permitted uses may occur in one or more of seven zones or categories. In addition to a use being permitted (or not permitted), it may be subject to limitation or require a special permit. For example, housing for the elderly is by special permit only in MF and commercial 1, 2, and 3; child day care center, by special permit in SF, permitted in MF and commercial 1, 2, and 3; post offices not permitted in SF and MF, by special permit in all other categories and zones.

As one might expect, industrial uses are confined to the industrial zones, but even here the appendix limits "establishments engaged in the manufacturing, fabricating, assembly, testing, repair, servicing, and processing" to those listed.[18]

Wholesalers of particular products are permitted only in the I-1 zone. There is provision for possible flexibility. The ordinance permits "any other use which the Planning Commission may find to be similar in character to the uses permitted in the specific zone or zones."[19]

The "Classical City"

The above examination of 12 cities reveals several interesting points, all relating to the conceptual notion of the classical city discussed in the beginning of this section. First, there are several aspects which are emphasized, perhaps overemphasized, by most of the 12 cities in their land-use policies. They range from attempts to create a 24-hour downtown, housing in downtown, and mixed-use development to preservation of neighborhoods. Examples of such attempts can be witnessed in Baltimore, Seattle, San Diego, Portland, Minneapolis, and Kansas City. One of the major attributes of the above policy is, of course, competition with suburbs for development of housing and retailing. Instead of searching for a new architecture for downtown, the cities attempt to bring the suburb to downtown. In doing so, they also attempt to revive the old city. Only one city attempted to deal with gentrification, Kansas City, and another city has gone as far as to create a quasi-pedestrian city, Vail.

The foundations of these land-use policies are, of course, economic development and creation of the old Heimlich (Homer) environment—a postmodern fever that attempts to mask the reality and then builds a wax museum.

5.2 BUILDING FORM

Building form has traditionally constituted the essence of zoning and urban design mechanism, as has been discussed earlier. It also has served as a commodity for the developer. The larger and more massive the building, the more square footage and, thus, the more profit per square foot of land. In crowded urban centers this push for square footage translates into an expansion in height. This important element, which forms the main content of architecture of the city, has been the subject of economic manipulation in exchange for so-called amenities such as plazas and arcades. Economic incentives are given to provide such amenities. These alterations and "improvements" should be as carefully thought out as other elements of the project. Gaining points is hardly a justification for a design decision.

It should be mentioned, however, that early attempts at regulating building form have been successful largely due to high-depth architectural analysis. A prime example is Hugh Ferriss's concept of high-rises in New York City subsequent to the 1916 zoning laws of the City of New York. Ferriss sets forth the stages of a building erected on a setback principle. A given mass is available to the architect that is the result of zoning laws translated into physical form. The mass is the "embodiment of legal rather than architectural concept," yet these concepts are based on both economic and public issues and thus embody human interest.[20] This brings up the other important and rational dimension of building form, the functional requirement for public health and safety pertaining to light, air, view, and other issues. For Ferriss these aspects of design helped to shape the initial mass that is given to the architect. This form is the "crude clay of the future city . . . imagined as already standing. There must come architects who, using the techniques of sculptors, will model the crude clay into the finished forms."[21] The zoning laws thus become vested with a physical form, the raw and essential material of the city.

The present state of building form in cities is mainly focused on several aspects with an attempt to follow the same direction as land use and an overall notion of the postmodern city. Compatibility and fit with the old structures of the city is the key determinant. Use of a similar architectural vocabulary and the incentive mechanism of public amenity are additional dimensions.

A powerful tool for the promotion of compatibility of structures both old and new is a guideline focus on preservation and historic district design. In the beginning, land-use policy and zoning laws tended to work against preservation. If a building was located in an area newly zoned for a different use, it was usually slated for destruction. However, land-use and zoning laws now work together with preservation to create the many "historic" districts to which we have referred throughout our discussion. This district focus, as mentioned earlier, has a great deal to do with building form as it tends to fragment the architecture of the city into pockets of style.

The preservation of whole districts and the strict codification of design for new structures within the area leads to "a new field for architecture and urban management: archiving, cataloging, preservation of historical monuments, and the reuse of existing structures built in the 20th century, those built recently, that are born useless."[22] Rossi finds this type of "contextual" preservation to be "counter to the real dynamic of the city. . . . [It] is related to the city in time like the embalmed corpse of a saint to the image of his historical personality."[23] The result is often quotation and analogy of existing style, a skin-deep acknowledgment of the context.

Nicolin sees this more as an outgrowth of an insecurity.

> The growth in the presence of analogy in contemporary architecture can be explained by this desire to establish a relationship of continuity with the "text" around us, and to ensure the legitimacy of our contribution by eliminating clashes and contrasts, to achieve a process of assimilation.[24]

Such concentration on preservation tends to be very one-sided. While romantic notions of Victorian charm continue to be perceived, anything old is preserved despite its original worth. The products of Modernism have become the evil side of the dialectical coin and are rejected. Zenghelis feels that

> by ignoring the reality of the world out there, (the real context), these proposals miss the point of architecture altogether: they do nothing to promote the betterment of this reality. Instead of ideas that relate to life, the public receives a lot of dogma for which it has little use.[25]

The common tool in the determination of building form is often FAR (floor area ratio). Some cities have even gone beyond these primary aspects and specify architectural details such as form and style, color and materials, and others. Seldom do cities deal with the issue of "siting" and "context" beyond the immediate physical boundary. Examination of our 12 cities will shed more light on this discussion.

Lincoln

There are no specific guidelines or policies for building form in Lincoln. However, the bylaws of Lincoln's Urban Design Committee include directives for review of city projects which indicate a concern for the

> relationship of masses and open spaces to assure that projects have been designed so that proposed masses and open spaces relate harmoniously to each other and to existing and planned development that may have a spacial or visual relationship to the proposed project.[26]

Portland

One of Portland's most distinctive city structures is its layout in small 200' by 200' blocks. The design commission wisely has advised continuation of this layout, and this recommendation has strongly affected building form and massing in Portland. The "Recommended Central City Plan" points out that "high density need not imply high rise development."[27] They compared two buildings of similar density and indicated that one, the Meier and Frank building, achieved higher density by having 12 floors equal in size. This document mentions that Portland's base FARs are higher than those in Seattle and San Francisco and similar to that of Minneapolis, to mention only the cities we are studying. Significant is the statement that a "number of these cities allow FARs higher than Portland's 15:1 if substantial public benefits are provided."[28] We should add that downtown Portland's existing FARs vary from 4:1 to 14:1.

Consultants and the Portland Chapter of the AIA originally recommended a height limit of 350 feet downtown as appropriate "to the 'Portland scale.'"[29] Then, in 1979, the maximum height was raised to 460 feet "with a step down in height between the office corridor and the river and lower heights around the south and west sides of public open spaces to ensure adequate light and air." There are lower height limits around historic districts, stepped-down heights toward the Willamette River, and height limits that protect view corridors. An expressed concern is that the 460-foot height limit might expand beyond the downtown, but "many of the height limits cannot be reasonably met under the maximum allowed FAR."[30] Finally, we note that an urban design goal of the "Recommended Central City Plan" is to "sensitively enhance Portland's human scale of buildings, streets and open spaces."[31]

Kansas City

Kansas City has perfected form and massing criteria, adapting them to specific situations in the city. For example, consider infill housing in residential zones of "The Plaza Urban Design and Development Plan." Bulk and form are

1. To provide appropriate transitions in scale to the adjacent residences . . . [and to observe] front, back and side yard setbacks.
2. For new construction, the building footprint and parking lot area should not exceed 75% of the building site. . . .
3. New apartment buildings should incorporate the form and architectural design elements of the single family residences that exist in the Plaza area.[32]

An issue of concern about general development in the Plaza area is that it "could damage the existing scale and character of the area."[33] Therefore, the urban design guidelines addressed several building form and placement concerns:

1. If a commercial development is to be located next to a residential zone, its height should not exceed 45 feet.
2. "The designs of future buildings should maintain the building placement and architectural features of the adjacent existing buildings."
3. In both commercial and residential areas, the established street walls are to be maintained, and building placement is to be similar to that existing around it.[34]
4. The developers of future buildings are to minimize bulk and mass by "articulation of the building form, step backs from the building base, plane changes within the building elevations and well-designed building facades."[35]

Within this single plan for the Plaza area, the City Development Department has recommended specific criteria for various problems of building form and massing. The idea of compatibility also can be found in regulations for an urban redevelopment district: "The height of any building or structure within the proposed district should be compatible with the land area and overall development. . . ."[36] Airport Zoning Map height limits are not to be exceeded either.

Indianapolis

Indianapolis also emphasizes compatibility and fit in its guidelines for Lockerbie Square Historic District. Note that these are but guidelines to be considered in renovation and repair, additions, and new construction. The building form and mass guidelines address setback, building heights, silhouette, orientation, spacing, and mass (Figure 5.1). General compatibility was also of concern in the Regional Center Zoning Ordinance. The Regional Center Plan covered many very different zones and emphasized districts, those already established and those proposed. The plan states that building form and massing can contribute to the definition of a district through "creation of distinctive homogeneous character [involving] building style, . . . proportion, . . . rhythm [and] scale" among other elements.[37]

An interesting facet of requirements in the Central Business District is the lack of height restrictions—except that no building may penetrate "Sky Exposure Plane Two" under ordinary conditions. One hundred percent lot coverage is permitted. If there are to be setbacks along a rear or side lot line that does not abut an alley, they must be at least ten feet wide.

Figure 5.1. Downtown Indianapolis from the southeast, a magnificent collage of surface parking and buildings. (*Source:* Indianapolis 1980-2000 Regional Center General Plan, 1981.)

Baltimore

Baltimore's district approach means different building form and massing requirements in each recognized district. In the "Inner Harbor Project I Renewal Plan" we find the following applicable measures:

1. No more than 250 residential units per net acre.
2. Each of 26 development areas has specific building coverage, setback, and elevation standards. For example, in commercial Development Area 11, the maximum permitted height is elevation 450 feet; up to grade level coverage, 100 percent; no building facade more than 270 feet south of the north property line.[38]
3. In Commercial Development Area 13, a maximum permitted height is but elevation 50 feet (with some specific exceptions by approval). Planning review by an ad hoc Advisory Task Force provides "citizen input into the design process for the improvements to be constructed . . . [with] final authority to approve or disapprove all proposed plans" reserved for the Department of Housing and Community Development.[39]

In the "Urban Renewal Plan, Charles North Revitalization Area," the final concern in the review of developers' plans for new construction by the Department of Housing and Community Development is "harmony of the plans with the surroundings."[40] Therefore, review is to include suitability of the site plan and elevations and conditioning of rear yard spaces. All this is in addition to the regular zoning requirements for the area.

The usages are mixed in the "Urban Renewal Plan, Washington Hill-Chapel." The requirements are quite specific. For example, in High Intensity Residential, the minimum lot size for a single-family detached house is 5000 square feet, with a maximum lot coverage of 40 percent. In a Community Commercial Area, commercial uses may have a FAR of 2.5; while in a Wholesale/Service Commercial Area, such uses may have a FAR of 4.0. Residential Disposition lots have minimum lot area, maximum lot coverage, maximum height, and minimum rear yard requirements for single-family attached and walk-up or elevator apartments. A maximum density of 30 dwelling units per net residential area is set.

San Diego

San Diego's zoning ordinances, in a manner similar to most cities, cover lot size, building placement, setbacks, height restrictions, etc. It is the special district ordinances that refine building form. San Diego has built in several layers of concern.

Building on the zoning ordinances, the "Urban Design Plan for Centre City San Diego" covers several districts and suggests

1. Siting new buildings so they don't block views from adjacent structures
2. Planning large developments so they won't form a "wall" restricting views
3. Designing buildings with architectural features that enhance views
4. Creating transitions in form and scale rather than abrupt changes
5. Scaling buildings to complement surrounding open space, e.g., terracing down to a waterfront or park area
6. Relating the form and scale of new buildings to those around them
7. Respecting the existing patterns of development, but seizing opportunities to vary—when the new structure will create a special plaza or pedestrian walkway, for example
8. Considering restoration rather than demolition, and repeating design characteristics of old buildings in new ones to bind an area together[41]

In 1987 an Urban Land Institute task force studied Centre City San Diego and made some pertinent suggestions about building form and massing.

1. Relieve the "rigid block configuration" by combining blocks and vacating streets to create new development areas and open space possibilities.[42]
2. In the marina area, allow "a range of densities [and] building heights."[43]
3. "Preserve the character, scale and architecture" of the Gaslamp Area with "rehabilitation/refurbishing of existing buildings."[44]
4. Establish development controls to include building height, bulk, and floor/area ratio regulations . . . [with] additional controls on view corridors, shadow and potential wind tunnel effect . . . for large scale projects" in the waterfront area.[45]

San Francisco

The 1984 downtown development controls, as a part of San Francisco's Master Plan, included height and bulk directives related to compatibility with existing structures. The idea was to construct new structures so as to blend in with the old rather than to overwhelm them. This is the pattern of controls that has been applied throughout San Francisco in an effort to preserve the city's uniqueness. The difficulty has been the subjective nature of many of the design directives. Copious illustrated examples guide the architect toward desired building characteristics: Avoid light-colored buildings because they stand out; a huge building on or near a hill is likely to mask the natural features of the area and block views; etc.

The committee that drew up the building guidelines for Bernal Heights East Slope castigated San Francisco's design principles, which were supposed "to assure that new development be compatible with the delicate scale and character of the existing housing in hillside residential areas."[46] These citizens looked around and saw boxes—perhaps dressed-up boxes, but still boxes—being built in their area. They speak of "relating a building to its topography," planning accessible yards for private open space, and stepping a building with the slope so that it does not lose "it[s] relationship with the ground."[47]

Other suggested techniques:

1. "Break up the overall massing into articulated architectural pieces."
2. "Require at least a partial 4'-0" wide sideyard on one side of the lot."
3. "Diminish height of the rear portion of the building."
4. "Get light, sun, air and views into and out of buildings."[48]

Seattle

The great variety of districts and neighborhoods in Seattle necessitates a variety of approaches to building form and massing. In the Ballard Avenue Landmark District, for instance, emphasis is on keeping the construction small, uniform in size, and, therefore, compatible with existing buildings. The preamble to the district guidelines sets the tone: "It is not intended to require the reproduction or recreation of earlier buildings, but rather to recognize their qualities of scale, proportion, size and materials."[49]

Seattle's goals for the Seattle 2000 Program has given the city an opportunity to examine all its policies and statutes closely to ascertain their effectiveness and desirability over the long haul. For example, the city undertook a "Seattle 2000 Action Inventory" to see how city actions between 1973 and 1984 were related to the goals. They found the following positive actions:

1. Regulations of heights in shoreline areas through the Shorelines Master Program
2. A new land-use code that measures height of buildings and sets locational criteria relating zoning to topography and adjacent areas to preserve and create view corridors[50]

In response to the Seattle 2000 goal that

building design must fit into a 3-dimensional downtown plan, views and access to sunlight must be considered before buildings are erected, [and] the traffic generating capacity of buildings must be considered before buildings are erected. [The city responds:] The Downtown Plan considers "3-dimensional" aspects (of the City) in proposed height limits, location of highest densities near major transportation corridors. . . .[51] (Figure 5.2)

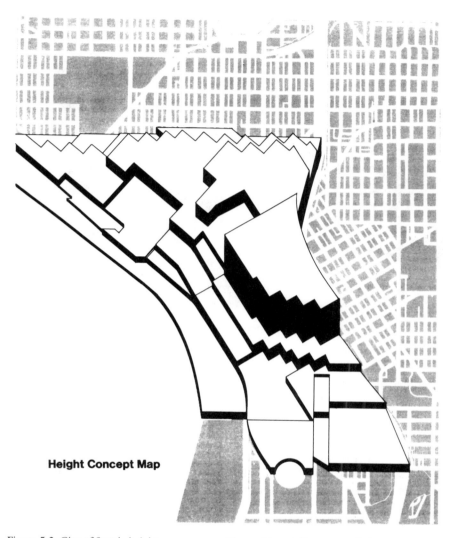

Height Concept Map

Figure 5.2. City of Seattle height concept map. (*Source:* Mayor's Recommended Land Use and Transportation Plan for Downtown Seattle, 1984, City of Seattle.)

Minneapolis

The "Metro 2000 Plan" in Minneapolis speaks of policies relating to building height and massing. While avoiding rigid design, it says that the emphasis should be on unity of development to give a sense of place—a complete district (Figure 5.3). The plan sees the strengths of downtown as "centrality,

Figure 5.3. An example of a downtown street in Minneapolis that is supposed to present a sense of place and unity.

completeness, and compactness."[52] Yet, the plan expresses the thought that "downtown architecture and urban design" should be concerned with "how buildings appear to pedestrians . . . [and] the skyline (particularly as viewed across the River and on the freeway approaches)." Optimistically, "the Plan formally introduces the concept of management as an essential means to achieve Plan objectives."[53] Zoning for downtown Minneapolis has been in place since 1963. The "Metro 2000 Plan" feels "that the current zoning pattern . . . has served admirably to produce an unusually dense core that supports retailing, skyways and public transit."[54] To keep zoning current, the plan recommends expansion of the denser areas "at certain points to meet the realities of growth" and revision of the bonus system.[55]

We're talking policies here, not the specifics of zoning; and Minneapolis does have zoning that prescribes building heights, massing, skyway connections, view corridors, etc. The problems that the Minneapolis Design Review Task Force saw in 1982 were potentials for overlap and delay, with review being done in several different city departments, and a lack of consistency—some reviews are binding, while others are but advisory. Their 1983 "Recommendations for a Design Review Process for the City of Minneapolis" never have been accepted despite their general nature. These recommendations spoke of mass, scale, and height relating to each other, "to their surroundings, and to the mass, scale and height of surrounding structures." Variety in height and scale should be used to "avoid too great mass and bulk." Design of height and mass should prevent creation of shadowing and relate "to ground/sidewalk level (and skyway level, if appropriate)." Massing, scale, and height are particularly important when a building is sited near a natural amenity. Transitions in scale should be noted near district boundaries.[56]

One wonders how many of these suggestions have been built into existing reviews or the zoning code, lacking complete city-wide design evaluation.

Irvine

Irvine attempts to create a diverse building form and, at the same time, a holistic city image. To begin, we can best discuss this within Objective B-2 of the Urban Design Element of Irvine's "General Plan": "Create a hierarchy of City components that consist of city, district, village, neighborhood, project and building scales." How is this to be done?

1. Utilize building masses, architecture and landscaping to create a sense of unity within variety for the various components of the city . . .
2. Distinguish villages in character and physical appearance from each other [by]

   — a mixture of housing types and densities . . .
   — physical compatibility with the local environment including topography . . .
   — a varied skyline . . .[57]

Residential Density Standards allow from less than 0.1 dwelling unit per acre (in rural areas) to the highest density, 25–40 dwelling units per acre. Natural conditions such as hillsides may lower allowed density. The standards for allowable density are not rigid; they may be mixed as long as the overall density does not exceed the allowed amount. A hillside village may have 2,000 to 10,000 residents, while flatland villages may have 5,000 to 30,000. Every aspect of development is planned and specified in advance to establish compatible uses and designs within a unit of housing, commercial development, or industrial use. Carefully landscaped areas provide smooth transitions from one use or area to another (Figure 5.4).

Dallas

Dallas's Central Business District indicates a good potential for great densification with an average FAR of 12:1. The only height limit mentioned is the approximate 50-story cap in the eastern CBD because of FAA regulations for

Dallas's Love Field. However, a zoning ordinance limiting heights to 100 feet will limit expansion at the west end of the CBD; and, of course, there is the Civic District to the south. Zoning presently allows a FAR of 20:1 for commercial development and 10:1 for residential. The existing residential setback requirements do not encourage residential development: one-half of the building height up to a maximum of 50 feet on all sides of the building. Since the city wants expansion of residential development in the CBD, these requirements could well be eased.

Dallas has more highly developed building height and massing regulations in historic and planned districts. Consider the West End Historic District, for example. Because many existing buildings are two to three stories, or 25 to 40 feet in height, the district wishes to preserve the "low-rise, boxy profile" with a height limit of 100 feet.[58] The "Near Eastside Conceptual Plan" (May 1984) sought creative reuse of old buildings and equal creativity in newly built buildings so that they will blend together well. The regulations retain the existing FAR of 4:1 because of the constraints imposed by street limitations. There is a height limit of 120 feet, no setback, and no coverage regulations. Accordingly, a developer can have "a 10:1 FAR building envelope within which to achieve a 4:1 FAR development and accommodate some or

Figure 5.4. An example of residential landscaping in Irvine. (*Source:* Bob Dannenbrink and Irvine Company.)

all of the required parking."[59] Bonuses for providing 50 percent residential units allow a FAR of 5:1 and a height of 140 feet.

Vail

Vail's form and massing requirements attempt to preserve view corridors. As Vail has grown, the core area of Vail Village has buildings of lower heights than the surrounding areas, a reflection of the bowl-shaped natural setting in a sense (Figure 5.5). There are no building setbacks specified; each development proposal is weighed separately for this aspect with such factors as compatibility with surrounding structures and streetscapes of influence (Figure 5.6). However, generally, no more than 80 percent of a site can be used for structures. The design of Vail Lionshead is less structured for presenting a unified image than is Vail Village.

Conclusions

Our discussion of the cities' building form presents us with underlying assumptions upon which guidelines regarding building form are developed: compatibility with surrounding building, harmony with existing structures, lower heights in historic districts, and FAR manipulations. We found exam-

Figure 5.5. A view of the composition of buildings with natural settings in Vail.

Figure 5.6. Another view from the core of the village where building height blocks mountain view, contradicting the ideas behind urban design policies.

ples in Lincoln, Kansas City, Portland, San Francisco, Minneapolis, Dallas, and Indianapolis. Several cities, Baltimore and Indianapolis, for example, differentiate among different parts of the city through district orientation. Some (Kansas City, Seattle, and San Francisco) go further into control of architectural detail. The only city that deals with "siting" and "building scale" and is flexible with existing structure is San Diego.

5.3 CIRCULATION AND PARKING

The automobile has had a major role in shaping most American cities from their inception, unlike most European cities. In America the street was created to anticipate future growth of the cities and did not develop from the *traces* of human activity.[60] Some streets in newer cities of the West never truly have had a pedestrian orientation; the city has grown up around the automobile, not its inhabitants. Thus, circulation and parking certainly hold important roles in the determination of the architecture of the city. The structure of highways, roads, and streets comes together to form the physical and formal layouts of cities.

At the present time, the cities' policies in regard to circulation and parking favor public transportation systems and a reduction of automobile usage in the downtown area, sometimes to the exclusion of proper maintenance of the existing infrastructure. American's roads, highways, and bridges are in critical shape. The abundance of open road and freedom of movement is something the average American citizen will not easily surrender.

Many cities' design guidelines tend toward a pedestrian-oriented downtown, a ban on automobiles in certain areas, and the building of parking garages that are buried or concealed. Many of these "pedestrianized" streets, however, were never meant for pedestrian scale and have no history as major corridors for pedestrian traffic. Hence, their success is limited. At the same time, most cities are moving toward expansion of public transportation. At a more focused level, the cities are concerned about the aesthetics of parking structures and parking for ground-level retailing that has created access space in many cities. Following is a substantive examination of the 12 cities' circulation and parking as it relates to architecture of the city.

Baltimore

Baltimore has a master plan for streets and highways and appropriates funds for bridge rehabilitation, repair, or replacement and for street highway reconstruction, rehabilitation, or resurfacing. Further, "the Interstate Division for Baltimore City . . . plans, designs, and constructs all Interstate Highways within Baltimore City."[61] Funds for alley and sidewalk paving come from city loans, city general funds, and the City Motor Vehicle Fund. The city pays for interstate joint development construction with monies from federal funds and from the City Motor Vehicle Fund. Add to the last sources funds from the state, "other funds," sale of city land, and county grants, and you have funds for the Interstate Division Construction Program. Highway construction money comes from a city loan, federal funds, and the City Motor Vehicle Department.[62]

Following all of the above street and highway allocations are 35 pages of planned expenditures for street lighting; footway and alley paving; repair of sidewalks damaged by tree roots; and widening, reconstruction, rehabilitation, resurfacing, demolition, and modification of specific streets, highways, and bridges. Over the years 1988–1993, arterial street reconstruction was to receive over $2 million from the City Motor Vehicle Fund, and that same fund was to provide over $2 million for roadway capacity and safety improvements such as left-hand lanes, corner radius increases, and median adjustments.

The Off-Street Parking Commission "oversees the development of parking facilities in the City to insure that new facilities are compatible with overall

City development objectives." It is parking in the downtown area and the city's core that is the target of policy decisions to provide

> competitively-priced alternatives [to all-day parking downtown] on the periphery of downtown [and to] selectively assist . . . private developers in the construction of parking facilities which complement redevelopment efforts.[63]

Projects were to include the Penn Station Garage/Plaza and three other parking garages at Inner Harbor East, Market Center, and Municipal Center. At the Inner Harbor West/Stadium area, parking facilities will serve the proposed stadium and provide parking for workers in and visitors to downtown.

Dallas

Dallas is hoping that the combination of its existing bus system and the new rapid transit system, DART, will ease congestion downtown and in other developing areas such as the special districts in the West End and La Avenida. The idea is to enable people to reach these areas, thus increasing activity and density without increasing traffic congestion. Dallas's special districts have incorporated circulation and parking elements. The Dallas Planning Department originally opposed keeping Market Street open, thinking that a pedestrian mall would be better. However, Michael Stevens, formerly with the Dallas Planning Department, later said: "Removing cars from Market Street and creating a pedestrian mall would have been the death of Market Street. Cars add vitality to the street—they bring exposure to the street and make it active and interesting."[64]

In contrast, 1981 plans for improvement to the Dallas Farmers Market spoke of optimizing "access to and within the Market area for pedestrians, automobiles and trucks."[65] Yet, the design guidelines state as one of the criteria for design of the market's physical improvements: "4. Establish well-defined edges to the expanded Market development and avoid the kind of motor vehicular penetrations existing today." Envisioned short-range needs included 100 more parking spaces and "improved vehicular circulation (through sheds and within parking lots)," while long-range needs were ever more (200–300) parking spaces ("possibly underground"), improved access via transit, and repeated efforts for better vehicular circulation.[66]

Underground parking was definitely a consideration in the Oak Lawn Plan and the La Avenida District. In the "CBD Concept Plan," transportation receives a deserved share of attention. Conceptually, the plan suggested subway connections and a grade-level strategy "to allocate circulation space according to these priorities: (1) pedestrians, (2) CBD shuttle transit, (3) regional line-haul transit, (4) delivery vehicles, and (5) private automobiles."[67]

Recommended were a core ring road to divert traffic from the core, a network of parking garages, upgrading of core streets for transit and pedestrians, and an improved CBD shuttle transit system.

San Diego

San Diego has taken serious steps to reduce traffic in Centre City by limiting the number of parking spaces that may be constructed per office unit. This is a far cry from the oft-taken approach of insisting on enough parking spaces to accommodate all workers/tenants (or payments in lieu of same), but it encourages/forces the use of public transit. Add to this the plans for some parking garages and a setting of street hierarchy (gateway streets and primary, secondary, and pedestrian streets), and you have a picture of a city that is serious about controlling traffic and willing to spend necessary funds on public transit by light rail and bus.

The 1983 "Urban Design Program, Centre City San Diego" planned to link developments with each other and with the waterfront with gateway streets in combination with pedestrian internal circulation linkages. A de-emphasis on on-street parking and the development of parking garages in Centre City and on the periphery were also plan policies. Intercity transit was the answer sought to bringing people from outside San Diego to Centre City, but transit also is necessary within Centre City.

Vail

We already have discussed Vail's policy to concentrate vehicles on the outer fringes of Vail Village (Figure 5.7). Nearly everyone who comes to Vail for skiing comes in a car, and finding a parking place in Vail Village had become a major problem. Presently, there is free bus service to and around the Village and a parking garage for Vail Village.

Vail's Zoning Code has a section on parking, and the Village's Master Plan has suggested other improvements:

1. Install traffic control systems at all entrances to the Village core to reduce vehicular traffic in the Village.
2. Limit delivery interference with pedestrians by setting times for delivery or by other means.
3. In order to make the greatest possible use of existing parking spaces in the Village, establish a leasing system.
4. All new development in the core is to contribute to a parking fund for new garages.

Figure 5.7. Although Vail's policy is to keep vehicles on the fringe of the city, one finds quite a few exceptions to the rule.

5. Encourage private shuttle vans and increase the free bus service as needed.

6. Expand the Transportation Center parking by 450 spaces.

Indianapolis

Zoning ordinances for the Central Business District of Indianapolis/Marion, County permit off-street parking garages with access(es) to the other streets in the CBD. Parking within buildings is permitted on the ground floor, providing that the space is no more than 25 percent of the gross floor area of the building and providing this parking is "incidental and accessory to the primary use or uses of the building."[68] Regulations for off-street parking lots require that the parking area be paved, that there be bumper guards to keep vehicles from extending into adjacent areas, and that lighting be shielded so it doesn't interfere with traffic or adjacent uses. Off-street loading space must be at least 500 square feet in area besides any maneuvering area provided. The number of off-street loading spaces required depends on the total adjusted net floor area in a specified ratio.

As long ago as 1981, when Indianapolis was developing its "Indianapolis 1980-2000 Regional Center General Plan," the city recognized that too many people were using their own cars to reach the downtown. While the street system was adequate to handle the traffic, certain street improvements were recommended to alleviate the problems of traffic congestion that had appeared on a spotty basis. At rush hour, the traffic was running at 60 percent of capacity; flex-time scheduling of employees would help with this. Car and van pooling and upgrading of arterial streets were other suggested measures.

Irvine

Circulation patterns are an important concept in Irvine's urban design scheme. Villages must be linked, and it must be very possible to get to the through-ways and to the industrial, commercial, and civic areas of Irvine (Figures 5.8 and 5.9). However, a major blockage in Irvine's effort to create a unified image is the freeways that cut through the city. There is concern expressed in the "General Plan" that villages will become internalized rather than relating to other villages and to the whole city. This is a probable reason for the emphasis on linkages.

Other cities, too, have adopted the idea of local streets vs. through streets. Irvine has perfected this approach with a multinodal system: residential villages, employment areas, and district centers. A "Street Design Manual and Standard Plans" (revised through December 1987) gives specifications, even speed limits varying from 25 mph on a local street to 60 mph on a major arterial. Irvine is a hillside city, so the specification that grades of more than 7 percent are not desirable is an interesting facet of compliance to standards.

"Westpark Design Guidelines" specify setbacks from parkways and Thiel Avenue to parking areas of 15 to 32 feet with screening required. There are certain streets throughout Westpark where there is to be no parking. Parking does not receive the attention in Irvine that it has in other cities we have studied because of the city's carefully orchestrated pedestrian walkway system and bicycle paths. The zoning code does set standards for parking.

Minneapolis

Zoning ordinances in Minneapolis permit off-street parking on a lot other than that of the building for which parking is required. However, the build-ing's owner must hold title to the other lot or have a long-term lease on it. In the R-1 through R-6 and the B-1 zoning districts, there is no parking allowed between the principal building and the front lot line. Each zoning district has its own regulations about the number of parking and loading spaces and

Figures 5.8. and 5.9. Two excellent examples of throughway design treatment in Irvine, California. (*Source:* Bob Dannenbrink and Irvine Company.)

accesses that must be constructed. Hotels, motels, and places of public gathering may gain a "premium" for planning off-street loading facilities and for off-street waiting facilities as well.

There are strict rules that apply to the reduced parking spaces allowed in connection with housing for the elderly and physically handicapped. A monthly report must be filed showing that no more than 10 percent of the tenants are below 60 years of age or not physically handicapped and that the number of cars in use, plus those operated by staff, does not exceed the number of parking spaces available. Break these rules and the zoning administrator can revoke the certificate of occupancy.

Minneapolis has been working on plans for Metro 2000 for 30 years already. As a result, there are some circulation and parking approaches in place.

1. To limit vehicular movement in the core, the external public transit system of buses and light rail vehicles brings people to the outer edges. Freeways feed commuters to a series of parking garages. Shuttle vehicles circulate in the core, and pedestrians move about freely. Actually, the transit system is to go right through the core so that riders can get off near their destinations.
2. Varying parking requirements push development to the center. There should be no long-term parking in the inner core. Within the ring of parking garages, parking should be provided by developers. Outside the ring, parking is the responsibility of buildings constructed there.
3. It is important to provide "circulator vehicles" to carry downtowners to and from the waterfront area.
4. Parking garages constructed over the Third Avenue North Distributor will keep commuter traffic off local streets.
5. The downtown has grown and developed; therefore, a transit system is important for providing conveyance between points too close to drive to but too far to walk.[69]

The aim of all this planning is to reduce the number of workers that commute by car from today's 45 percent and the number of similar commuting shoppers from 79 percent—no small undertaking.

Kansas City

Circulation is a concern in Kansas City's Plaza Area because the primary traffic arterials carry traffic through the area as well as feed the secondary and collector streets. So far, the three-, four-, and six-lane arterials are handling the traffic rather well except at peak traffic hours. Bus service is also available along the arterials.

There are some problems:

1. The principal intersection at Main and 47th Streets is overtaxed at peak traffic hours.
2. The breaks in the north-south arterials (caused by topography, early street decisions, and Brush Creek), as well as east-west problems, will lead to access problems generally as traffic increases.
3. Some secondary streets are already overtaxed.
4. Older apartment buildings do not have adequate parking.
5. Travel speeds on some arterial streets are below 25 mph now, with 25 mph a desirable speed for arterials.

The planners of the Plaza Area conclude that traffic and transportation problems could limit development in the future. Shared parking facilities, particularly by apartment tenants and commercial parking garages, are going to be essential. "While the Plaza has been assuming many of the functions of a downtown, it has not been supported by the kind of access system that a downtown needs."[70] The Plaza Plan suggests major improvements in east-west and north-south accesses, retention of the rail right of way for future rapid transit access, and improved bus service. Developers in the Plaza Area already contribute to roadway improvements, and this policy should continue for future developers.

As in Minneapolis, each zoning district in Kansas City has its own parking or parking and loading regulations. Some residential districts allow no truck parking except for deliveries or for vehicles of 20 feet or less that are owned by the resident and kept for personal use. In general, off-street parking should be located on the lot of the building it services. However, as in some of the other cities, an adjoining or nearby lot may be used for parking. Many of the districts require that the off-street parking area be in the rear or side yard of a property. The screening off and paving of parking areas is required. Kansas City also recognizes auxiliary parking for customers and employees in its zoning ordinances. This type of parking may be a parking lot or a parking garage of not more than three stories. Shared use of parking for residences, churches, and nonprofit groups by commercial uses is allowed.

Seattle

The goals set in 1972–1973 in Seattle 2000 provide strong support for public transportation, but how do the citizens of Seattle react now to issues involved in circulation? The results of a phone and *Seattle Times* survey indicate a high degree of agreement with the 1972–1973 goals; the support for public transportation has continued.[71]

In 1984 the Seattle City Council adopted some rather restrictive "Land Use Policies for Neighborhood Commercial Areas." Several "Commercial Area Development Standard Policies" are of interest in the present discussion; there are rules for drive-in business, heavy traffic generators, required off-street parking, location and design of parking, loading facilities, and light and glare control. Without our going any further, the reader would be correct in assuming that Seattle wants to control circulation and parking in neighborhood commercial areas.

Space does not permit us to discuss all aspects of these policies. The "Drive-In Business Policy" indicates the direction of council's thinking:

> Development standards for drive-in businesses and accessory drive-in facilities are established in order to minimize traffic impacts and pedestrian-vehicle conflicts, avoid disruption of an area's business frontage, and improve the appearance of the commercial area.[72]

Beatrice Ryan has called transportation in Seattle "a key element of the downtown policies which lower . . . densities and heights where the new transit system would not support large numbers of employees. . . ." Later she observes that "the downtown proposals required a massive investment in transit at a time when federal assistance is uncertain."[73]

Portland

Portland has a long history of attention to circulation and parking problems. Dedicated in 1978, the Transit Mall focuses busing activity and improves service for the public. Like Irvine, Portland has a carefully orchestrated street hierarchy. There are principal avenues with minor cross streets and accentuation of bridgehead entrances. The city has established the Arterial Street Classification Policy (ASCP), in place since 1977, which "recognizes the street right-of-way as one of the most valuable resources controlled by the city" and has the goals of "providing efficient movement for people and goods and protecting the livability of Portland."[74]

Studies for the "Recommended Central City Plan" revealed how much of certain parts of downtown was taken up by parking. For example, in the Coliseum/Lloyd Center District, 29 percent of the district is devoted to surface and structured parking, not unusual, one would suppose, for an area with large public gathering places. In the downtown and north of Burnside districts, the applicable figure is 13 percent for "parking lots, structures and personal vehicle uses."[75] It is significant that the plan includes surface parking lots in the "parcels considered to have redevelopment potential."[76] Where will people park, or will they use mass transit? The answer is found in a section called "A Vision of the Central City in the Future." The planners visualize a "diverse transportation system: A regional light rail system, parking for those that need it, trolley lines, water taxis, walking and bicycling."[77]

Lincoln

Lincoln does not appear to have a policy or plan in place in regard to circulation and parking. The city is concerned with parking projects and their appearance, in particular, in reference to several projects such as Centerpointe.

San Francisco

While San Francisco is emphasizing expansion of its mass transit to discourage single-occupant commuting automobiles, the city has made plans for improvement of the parking situation. Some may not see "improvement" when the policy of no increase in parking in the downtown is mentioned. But expansion and extension of bus and ferry service, Caltrans, Bay Area Rapid Transit (BART), San Francisco Municipal Railway (MUNI), and Metro, including more internodal connections, should ease congestion in San Francisco, particularly downtown. San Francisco has had a "transit first" policy since 1973.[78] Remember San Francisco's office limitation policy which we already have discussed at some length? One of the factors used in the "suitability of a development for its location" is "transit accessibility. How close is the project to local and regional transit?"[79]

In evaluating transit accessibility, the following scale will be used:

Excellent: Within easy walking distance (defined as ¼ mi) to regional transit carriers and many MUNI lines.

Good: Within reasonable walking distance (defined as ¼ to ⅓ mi) to regional transit carriers and major MUNI routes.

Fair: Within maximum walking distance (defined as between ⅓ and ½ mi) to regional transit carriers and major MUNI routes.

Poor: Exceeds maximum walking distance (defined as beyond ½ mi) to regional transit carriers and major MUNI routes.[80]

Also rated are "conflicts with transit, traffic or pedestrian movements [and] impediment to freight loading."[81]

The figures compiled in "Downtown" have had the desired effects on the office limitation policy. It will be revealing to learn how expansion can continue downtown without increasing parking there, without freeway or bridge expansion, and with no extension of "peak hour flow" with staggered work hours. By 1987, MUNI planned a 15 percent expansion and BART, 37 percent.[82] Longer-term parking is to be expanded beyond the core. "Downtown" suggests that new parking structures should be located carefully to make maximum use of transit and shuttle busing and that preference and incentives be given to vans and carpools.

Conclusions

The above discussion has highlighted several attitudes presently dominating the American city. The automobile is the enemy. Keep cars out of the city *or* allow them to its edge. Build parking structures but bury them, hide them, screen them, or give them a compatible facade. Move towards public transportation to alleviate the car crunch.

Only one city out of 12 appears to be concerned about maintenance and taking steps towards a solution—Baltimore. Only one city has been able to create a pedestrian city—that is Vail, obviously. All cities are concerned about parking and amenities in the parking areas: lighting, landscape, signage, etc. Interestingly enough, there are only a few cities attempting to deal with an American city and accept *cars* as the main means of transportation and deal with circulation and parking in an integrative way with architecture. Irvine is a prime example; San Diego is another, while Indianapolis and Minneapolis have, to some extent, taken steps toward it. None of the cities, however, has taken full advantage of parking structures and surface parking as artifacts essential in the American city. There is a clear conflict between re-creating the city of the past and dealing with the present. The modern city was based in part on vehicular activity. You may reject Modernism, but you cannot deny the reality of the automobile when it still remains in the city.

5.4 LANDSCAPE

The term landscape has come to mean something quite different than its original term in German, *landschaft*. Once it was seen as the opposite of the untouched wilderness, a manipulation of the land; now it has become somehow akin to the natural environment.[83] It is both nature and the man-made brought together in an attempt to reconcile them both, a "new naturalness in an unnatural state."[84] Landscape is a significant part of architecture, for it is the context within which the object is placed. The architecture of the city is, therefore, a collage of context and objects where the context is the city landscape and open space, and objects are buildings and structures.

The fundamental problem, however, is that many cities deal with this landscape content area as a functional and beautification element rather than as an integrated contextual element. Most policies, plans, and guidelines deal with natural landscape and not landscape built and natural. We also have seen that economic incentives are used to encourage the space but not the quality of the space. Landscape is treated as a separate issue, an afterthought, and is not given the same scrutiny as the architecture that inhabits it. The edge of the built form is severe, and the landscape beyond is a "wasteland, something neither private nor public, neither beautiful nor ugly."[85] Some cities studied, such as Seattle and Dallas, give points for public improvements including public open space within the urban environment. It is important to remember, however, that "space does not become public by merely ceasing to be private, or by being provided in quantities that no private purpose requires."[86] The evidence of this can be seen in the deserted urban squares and public areas.

Let us review our 12 cities to examine the scope of elements covered under this content area.

Dallas

Dallas discovered that landscape and open space were important elements of the architecture of the city in reconstruction of the West End district. Streetscape and amenities provided green spine along the historic corridors with a plaza at the end. There is a different emphasis in the "CBD Concept Plan" for Dallas. Here we find reference to

> urban spaces: a system of public parks, grade-level pedestrian ways, privately-developed (but publicly-accessible) plazas and courtyards, landscaped boulevards, and publicly-accessible interior spaces such as building atria and through-block lobbies.[87]

Dallas recognizes the need to make use of all opportunities for open space in its intensely developed downtown. The acceptance of "Landscaping Regulations" for the entire city (with some exceptions) is a major step toward a cohesive architecture of the city. Ordinance 18968 amended Chapter 51 of the "Dallas Development Code" by adding a new Article X in December 1985. This was a practical approach: "The economic base of the city can and should be protected through the preservation and enhancement of the unique natural beauty, environment, and vegetative space in this area."[88]

One of the purposes of the ordinance was "to provide visual buffering between land uses of differing character."[89] The ordinance encourages the creation of pedestrian facilities, "publicly accessible . . . plazas, covered walkways, fountains, lakes and ponds, seating areas and outdoor recreation facilities" and awards up to five points to the architect planning such amenities.[90] Since a project must accrue a certain number of points in order to receive approval from the building official prior to commencing work, the points for open space can become important to the architect.

Baltimore

Baltimore is expending considerable funds for parks and recreation. Referring again to "Baltimore's Development Program, 1988–93," we note that a total of over $6.5 million is anticipated for the development, improvement, and restoration of parks.[91] Quality public housing is one of the goals of the Neighborhood Progress Administration. The city proudly points to the "parklike atmosphere near the main entrance to Allendale," one of the public housing projects integrated with landscaping and amenities.[92] The Neighborhood Incentive Program helped residents of the Wilson Park Neighborhood rescue land planned as housing for use as a park/playground instead. In the Fels Point Neighborhood, the city has made good on its promises of public access to the waterfront with a paved promenade that stretches to the Inner Harbor.

Vail

Vail's policy is to preserve the natural landscape by concentrating development in the central corridor and to protect the view corridor, moves marked by some degree of success. The Town of Vail originally adopted design considerations for Vail Village and Lionshead in 1980. These "guideline design parameters" have continued to be of influence.[93] The preeminent importance of pedestrianization led to its being discussed first in the "Vail Village Design Considerations." The town wanted to improve the quality of the walking experience [by] open space and landscaping . . . along those routes."[94] And later: "It is desired to have a variety of open and closed spaces, both built and landscaped, which create a strong framework for pedestrian walks as well as visual interest and activity."[95]

San Diego

Though Mid-City San Diego has had a community plan since 1965, it was not until 1984 that the city completed a major overhaul of this plan. The situation was critical, with a few canyons as the only surviving open space. The city welcomed a state proposal to cover a full block of the proposed I-15 freeway, thus providing a four-acre park for Mid-City. The state also agreed to improve two other park sites. The "Mid-City Community Plan" proposed that the city acquire all remaining open space, largely canyons, slopes, and floodways. Restrictive zoning would "ensure a development intensity consistent with the topography."[96] Further, the plan suggests the use of TDRs "to protect open space and encourage infill in the appropriate locations."[97] Accesses to usable public open space would make passive recreation possible for San Diegans. A final recommendation would allow planned residential developments with "designated open space . . . a credit of a dwelling unit per acre in such areas."[98]

During discussion of a proposed overlay ordinance for Centre City San Diego in May 1986, the subject of seating in plazas was mentioned. The original statutory text suggests "one linear foot of seating for each 30 square feet of plaza area" in plazas of 1000 square feet or more. The various interested parties—San Diegans, Inc., the Central City Association, the San Diego Chamber of Commerce, downtown residents, and Citizens Coordinate for Century 3—all seemed open to further development of plaza standards. The City Planning Department stated: "Plaza standards are proposed as a means of addressing all other street level landscaping [except surface parking]. The Department recommends reducing seating ratio."[99]

Portland

Portland's expansive "Central City Plan" includes recommended actions for increasing open space along the Willamette River, particularly on the east bank where more space is needed for nonvehicular usages. Also seen as important was increased public access to the water and making sure the bridges would foster pedestrian and bicycle connections between banks of the river. Another grand plan for Central City is "a park and open space system of linked facilities that tie the Central City districts together and to the surrounding community."[100] The idea is to improve existing parks, make sure each district has appropriate open space, balance passive and active outdoor activities, and use presently available open space near housing for temporary community gardens. The plan also recognized that grain elevators now in use might stop operations someday. The land they occupy then should become public open space.

Zoning changes in the Northwest Triangle Area would provide for "open area: . . . sheltered or unsheltered walkways, paths, plazas and landscaped features or areas." The ordinance change specifically excludes any parking areas or landscaped areas near parking areas from being considered as open space. "A minimum of 25% of the required open area must be devoted to one primary gathering space," and no more than 25 percent of the open area can be walkways.[101] "Amendments to the Recommended Central City Plan" (March 1988) included a "study and report on the feasibility of constructing an elevated park over the freeway from the Burnside Bridge south and from the river to First Avenue." The suggested schedule for construction was over the next five years, and private funds might be necessary to supplement those from Parks, Planning, and the Department of Transportation.

Seattle

"Equal access to open space for all citizens" was one of the original Seattle 2000 Goals; indeed, it has been retained as "a locational criterion in multi-family housing."[102] The city has taken action to protect lakes, shorelines, and streams and has included the concept of public access to these natural amenities as important. The Adopt-A-Park program enlists citizens to help maintain neighborhood parks, and the P-Patch program encourages community gardens on vacant land, another manifestation of open space policy.

There are plans for major new downtown urban spaces, open space in new public projects, and street parks. The "Mayor's Recommended Land Use and Transportation Plan for Downtown Seattle" also recommends urban plazas, parcel parks, public and shopping atriums, rooftop gardens, hillside terraces, and voluntary building setbacks to gain some open space. But the "Summary of Land Use and Transportation Plan for Downtown Seattle" (1985) devotes a single paragraph to parks and open spaces with mention of some of the types of open space above now listed as "floor area bonus system public benefit features."[103] There is certainly a mixed message in regard to landscape and open space.

Lincoln

There appear to be no official policies or plans in regard to landscape and open space in Lincoln except some studies completed by a mayor's ad hoc committee. They recognized that the single project by the Taubman Company cannot meet all downtown open space needs. Rather it should emulate the Plaza in Kansas City, an "urbane melding of inside and outside."[104]

San Francisco

San Francisco's Downtown Plan, adopted by the City Planning Commission as a part of the Master Plan for San Francisco in November 1984, provides that an architect must "use at least $2 per square foot of new construction to create open spaces—public parks and malls."[105] This Downtown Plan aims to prevent the shadowing of a plaza as caused by the Bank of America Building constructed in 1969. TDRs will encourage open space development at some downtown sites "in exchange for certain planning exemptions at other sites."[106]

Unlike Seattle, San Francisco presents a unified message and stresses "providing adequate open spaces" in its very first objective of the "City-Wide

Land Use Plan," a part of the "Land Use Section of the Master Plan."[107] This idea is reinforced by the first principle of the Land Use Plan:

> The natural division of the city into two distinct functional areas—one primarily for production, distribution and services and the other for residential purposes and the community facilities which are closely related to residential activities. . . .[108]

Later, the plan speaks of providing land for public and commercial facilities "in proportion to the prospective population which will obtain under the standards of the citywide Land Use Plan."[109]

Finally, the Master Plan clearly recognizes the many types of open space and presents guidelines for urban gardens, urban parks, plazas, view and/or sun terraces, greenhouses, snippets ("small sunny sitting space[s]"), atriums, indoor parks, public sitting areas in galleries and arcades, and pedestrian walkways.[110]

Indianapolis

Indianapolis's "1980-2000: Regional Center Plan" states that it will provide "an opportunity for recreations, entertainment and tourism, . . . an attractive environment for people to live, work and play."[111] Where does open space fit into this plan? It is not listed as such in the Plan Summary; but in the Goals and Objectives we learn that the Regional Center already has 40 acres of downtown parkland of value to recreation and tourism.[112] Next, let us examine the section on urban design to see if there is discussion of open space needs. A good sign: The first item discussed is nodes, defined as "small homogeneous areas that are the focus of activity." Through the discussion that follows, we discover that nodes have "people . . . passing through, stopping, meeting, eating lunch, visiting." Additionally, indoor/outdoor related activities "generate activity beneficial to the vitality of nodes."[113]

Kansas City

It is useful to examine the proposed "City Plan" that was under discussion in the Kansas City Planning Department in September 1987. This new plan calls for the following:

1. "Open spaces and park lands that are adjacent to or integrated in urban centers must be maintained and uses coordinated in all future planning efforts."[114]
2. With regard to the Missouri River: ". . . Identify locations for public parks and look for opportunities to purchase this land."[115]

3. "Make the Missouri River downtown a major recreational attraction by promoting the location of major public facilities and events."[116]
4. "Encourage land uses along river banks that complement parks and other public uses and facilities"; e.g., a marina.[117]
5. "An attractive physical setting, organized around parks, boulevards and waterways and with quality public facilities . . . enhances quality of life."[118]
6. Open space and streetscape, pedestrian circulation and linkages between subareas are among the items that will "improve the visual appearance of downtown."[119]
7. "Green" the downtown with a "major downtown tree planting program [and] downtown green spaces."[120]

Though the Plaza area already has numerous public parks and boulevards, there is concern about repeated flooding along Brush Creek, overuse of Loose Park and a continuing need for improvements there, and underuse of other parks. Opportunities exist in the Plaza area for unified pedestrian walkways and jogging trails which will need enhancements. Open space in preservation areas is important and includes small parks, streetcar shelters, and tennis courts.

The urban design guidelines for the Plaza area set standards for open space:

1. Projects with less than 20,000 square feet of area must have ten percent of the area as greenspace or public plaza; larger projects, more than 20,000 square feet, must have 20 percent.
2. A public plaza or greenspace must include 40 linear feet of seating space; i.e., benches or low walls.
3. A buffer zone with landscape screening is necessary between commercial and residential areas.[121]

Irvine

The Land Use element in Irvine's Comprehensive Plan describes all land uses, including open space, in some detail. Of course, we already know that open space is important to The Irvine Company's plans for the city with open space as a buffer between differing uses, as a means of turning streets into boulevards, for conservation, and for large and smaller public facilities. Open space spines connect the villages to each other and to other usages; there are bicycle and equestrian trails; in laying out roadways, the city has strategically located scenic lookouts. After all, Irvine is a planned combination of flatland and rolling hills.

For general public use, the city has regional parks, wildlife habitat areas and preserves, and nature centers. A park may also be a part of a multiuse area corridor. There are public and private lakes and golf courses. Open space is also an important part of each village, with smaller community parks of 20 acres or less plus nearby school property, trails, and greenbelt areas. Exclusively agricultural land is still a designated use in Irvine, and development reserve is presently agricultural and accessory residential land which must be rezoned before development can begin.

Irvine guards its hill areas closely, allowing limited development and reserving natural landscape, particularly wildlife and natural habitat. A marsh is another wildlife area, again with only some development permitted. The City of Irvine has adopted a Conservation and Open Space Plan, indicating its resolve to protect such areas. The city maintains a data base cataloging natural features. This latter activity is also important for determining hazardous areas unsuitable for development because of soil shifting, possible earthquake damage, slopes, or floodways. Despite the seeming abundance of open space, Irvine plans to make use of closed landfill areas for recreational use.

Minneapolis

"Metro 2000 Plan," the latest update of Minneapolis's look toward the year 2000, dwells on the concentration of people, events, and economic activity in the downtown. Therefore, open space, too, is seen as full of people. "Within the core, the human scale of pedestrians should dominate."[122] Aiming toward flexible planning for all usages, landscape and open space must "be enhanced, made more inviting and integrated with pedestrian pathways."[123]

This will be accomplished by softening paved areas with grass, adding seating, and encouraging gathering by making the paths themselves interesting with vistas and small landscaped areas. If people are going to return to the inner city to live, the surroundings have to be inviting, open, and safe. Families with children particularly need accessible open space. Along the riverfront, public access and open space are essential to nearby residential development and public use.

Conclusions

The above discussion reveals several dimensions of landscape and open space in our 12 cities. Most deal with these aspects as functional/aesthetic means and not essential context, with the exception of San Diego, and San Francisco and Irvine to some extent. Again, very few deal with issues of open space and environmental conservation, ecology, and natural resources. San Diego and Irvine are again among these few.

5.5 SIGNAGE

Baltimore

Baltimore has been concerned with signage since 1967, as reflected in the provisions set forth in the "Inner Harbor Project I Renewal Plan" (dated from June 1967 onward). In review and approval of signs, the Agency (Charles Center Inner Harbor Management) "will be concerned with, but not limited to, size, design, illumination, location, materials, color, and method of installation."[124] The Agency must approve all lighting of signs, structures, etc. These directives are included in but two short paragraphs.

By the time the urban renewal plan for the Charles/North Revitalization Area was approved in October 1982, the provisions for the review of signs were changed. Now the Department of Housing and Community Development was to consult with the Charles North Community Association on "materials and design of all signs."[125] Then follows about a page and a half of specific provisions about signage and lighting. Nonconforming signs are to be removed within two years, but no penalty for nonremoval is found within the ordinance. Despite this apparent concern about signage, the subject is not emphasized at all in "The Development Guide Book: Requirements for Building in Baltimore City" (third edition, April 1985).

Dallas

Dallas appears to have devoted a high level of energy to regulating signs. The city first passed a sign ordinance in 1978 and revised it in 1980, 1981, and 1983 (Figure 5.10). All nonconforming signs are supposed to have been removed; but compliance has not been universal, and some billboards are still in evidence. The departments of Housing and Neighborhood Services and of Planning and Development have published a "Sign Manual: Interpretive Materials for Sign Regulations" (1983, Publication No. 8301018). While a disclaimer warns the reader to consult the sign ordinance itself for definitive regulations, the booklet also includes explanatory footnotes to the ordinance, illustrative examples, and applicable building code provisions.

Without delay, an architect should be able to ascertain the applicable restrictions on his or her project. There are specific requirements for each district: business, nonbusiness, special provisions, and the CBD-Freeway Loop Zoning District. Architects can carefully study the ordinances, then consult the proper illustrations and determine the electrical, design, and construction standard in force. The illustration section is organized helpfully with, for example, a roughly sketched drawing of "maximum projection,"

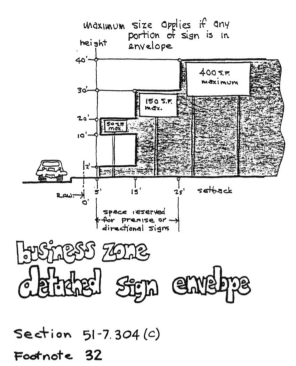

maximum size applies if any
portion of sign is in
height   envelope

Section 51-7.304 (c)
Footnote 32

Figure 5.10. An example of signage requirements in Dallas. (*Source:* Sign Manual, 1978, City of Dallas.)

followed by a citation of the applicable section in the ordinance and mention of any pertinent footnotes.

Indianapolis

Applications for approval of new construction, changes in intensity of use, and exterior remodeling in the Regional Center of Indianapolis must include information on signs, including such details as elevation, location, size, copy, design, illumination, color, and materials. Similar information is required for approval of signs in Indianapolis's Special Districts: hospital, park, university quarter, commercial, market square, and Central Business, and in planned unit developments.

Design standards for the Lockerbie Square Historic District are quite specific about recommended characteristics. These are, of course, guidelines, not absolute requirements; but the "Staff of the Indianapolis Historic Preservation Commission is available to help interpret the criteria established by the standards and assist in finding appropriate approaches for the development of projects."[126] The standards ask architects to "avoid internally lit . . . [and] free-standing signs, . . . billboards, . . . signs concealing architectural details," and those having "a negative impact on surrounding residential buildings." A particularly interesting requirement is that "signs identifying a home occupation, historic information or neighborhood association membership should not . . . constitute advertising."[127] Nevertheless, these design standards for signs call on reviewers to use discretion in their considerations for approval.

Irvine

The Land Use Element of Irvine's "General Plan" declares that billboards (and strip commercial and polluting industries) are "non-harmonious with Irvine."[128] When we also learn that the villages are encouraged to establish signage regulations to ensure compatibility, we can surmise that signage will be quite extensively regulated. A further indication is the stringent sign ordinance.

If a development has two or more businesses or five or more temporary and/or permanent signs or includes a historic structure or wall signs on buildings more than two stories high, the City of Irvine requires a "sign program." This will make it more certain the signs satisfy the sign ordinance's intent that they

> are in harmony with, and visually related to: a. Other signs in the sign program; b. The building and/or development they identify; c. Surrounding development. . . . The Sign Program must consist of graphic representation of all proposed signs and written regulations governing the location, size, color, style and illumination of the signs. The sign program must feature several common design elements to unify all on-site signs.[129]

Kansas City

In Kansas City, as in most of the other cities, signage near or in residential areas is of concern and is closely controlled. Otherwise, signage regulations depend on an area's land uses, zoning controls, or a building's size and height. Once these matters are specified, location and spacing are also considered. Again, as in other cities, special districts have special signage controls.

In the Plaza area, for example, the urban design guidelines suggest "similar signage location" on new structures so that they will be more compatible with existing structures.[130] The infill housing urban design regulations require that signs identifying multifamily residential units "be wall flushmounted, located above the building entry and below the second story windows with a maximum size of ten square feet."[131] Each section of the Plaza area that will be developing has its own specific signage regulations reflecting the particular conditions and expected development. This means that there may be no wall-mounted signs above the second story in some districts, but in others these signs may be mounted on the third story. The Plaza plan anticipates that the zoning ordinance must be amended in order that pole-mounted signs can be forbidden in a section of the northeast quadrant. In another section of the northeast quadrant, the signage regulations attempt "to improve the visual continuity . . . through uniformity in the size and placement of signs."[132]

Lincoln

Lincoln-Lancaster County has recognized signing as one of "several projects [that] should be undertaken to review standards being applied in the areas in terms of their impact on the quality of design."[133]

Minneapolis

Minneapolis does have a sign ordinance. In business districts alone there are 15 listings of specific regulations for signs. The architect must become quite well acquainted with these rather extensive provisions. For example, consider the restrictions of projecting signs: The provisions of the zoning code limiting such signs do not apply to "identification canopy or marquee signs indicating only the name of the building or the name of the principal occupant. . . ."[134] The size of the lettering "may not exceed 16 inches in height, . . . except that in a B4 District, the upper case or capital letters and the upward or downward extensions of any lower case letters in a script sign may not exceed thirty-six (36) inches in height. . . . "[135]

The manufacturing and residence districts, Minnesota Technology Corridor, riverfront development generally, and service stations all receive special attention as far as signage is concerned. Even political candidates need to know their way through the maze of sign regulations. While such signs are allowed in all districts, they may not be placed on public property or on private property "where otherwise prohibited."[136]

Portland

Portland also has design requirements for signage which call for compatibility with the existing architecture in historic districts. The Landmarks Commission must review all proposed new or replacement signs. In the Chinatown and Broadway districts, however, ornate, large, brilliantly lighted signs are acceptable because they will fit in with the splashy oriental and entertainment atmospheres. If properly maintained, banners, flags, and paper ornaments are permitted in Chinatown; they will be reviewed for appropriateness every six months.

Because the Central Eastside Area of Central City Portland is an industrial area, use of the recommended "proposals for action" in the "Recommended Central City Plan" will aid access: "Improve marking of truck routes to and through the district," a directive to the city itself.[137] There do not appear to be any significant changes in signage regulations in Central City Portland's plan. This may be because the existing design review application requirements include regulation of signs and provide for the review of signs alone or as a part of site review. Portland wants to have signs fit in with other aspects of a project and with the streetscape as well. Adjustments in requirements are possible if "the spirit and intent of the objectives of these regulations would best be served by the issuance of such a permit."[138]

San Diego

San Diego has regulated signs visible from public ways since 1973. The Regulatory Planning Division of the San Diego Planning Board reviews signage and enforces the ordinance. In Old Town San Diego, a historic district, there can be no billboards. Though the "Urban Design Program, Centre City San Diego," speaks again and again of improving visual quality while allowing for diversity, the booklet does not specially deal with signage.[139] By 1987, the provisions of the Centre City Overlay Zone required a signage program for any new or renovation project costing $250,000 or more for construction. Special prohibitions include inflatable displays on roofs, signs more than 65 feet above the sidewalk, and logos on two adjacent facades. The size of an allowed logo is computed in relationship to the height of the building on which it will be used.

San Francisco

Permits for signs are required by Article Six of San Francisco's *Zoning Code*. Additionally, in the discussion of historically significant and contributory buildings in conservation districts, signs

> may be disapproved, or approved subject to conditions, if the proposed location, materials, means of illumination or method of replacement of attachment would adversely affect the special architectural, historical or aesthetic significance of the building or the Conservation District. No application shall be denied on the basis of the content of the sign.[140]

San Francisco has had an abiding concern for visual harmony, expressed in its "Master Plan" as avoiding "extreme contrasts in color, shape and other characteristics which will cause new buildings to stand out in excess of their public importance."[141] Is signage one of those "other characteristics?" This has not been discussed specifically, but it is in keeping with San Francisco's relying on guidelines. Later, there is reference to "visual interest of street facades."[142] The city must feel that the provisions of Article 6 are adequate for controlling signage.

At last, under "Fundamental Principles for Neighborhood Environment" in the "Master Plan," we find:

> Dignified and well-maintained signs designed with respect for the scale and character of the street can enhance commercial areas. When signs do not relate to the area, when they reach excessive size, and when they feature blatant and discordant designs, they reflect poorly upon the overall quality of a commercial area.[143]

Again, glittering generalities to confuse the architect rather than guiding with specifics.

Seattle

Signage proposals in city projects get the scrutiny of Seattle's Design Commission on a project-by-project basis city-wide. Each historic or special district has its own design review board or commission to handle signage. For example, in the Pike Place Market District, regulations forbid certain types of signs, while the commission has some latitude in granting permission for temporary signs and banners.

In the Pioneer Square Preservation District, the following signs are prohibited:

Permanently affixed, free-standing signs (except those used to identify areas such as parks)
Roof signs
Billboards
Electric signs, excluding neon signs[144]

The preservation board also encourages building owners to develop a signage program.

In judging signs, the board considers the following aspects:

1. Suitability of the sign's texture, colors, and graphics in relationship to those of the building and other signs
2. Possibility of damage to a structure by erecting the sign
3. Compatibility of the sign with the character of the building

The ordinance also sets standards for the size of signs and for signing on awnings, canopies, or marquees. "Historic precedent, locational or visibility concerns of the business" can influence decisions on "projecting signs, neon signs, signs which appear to be in motion and signs with flashing, running or chaser lights."[145]

In establishing a signage policy for commercial areas, Seattle realized that neighborhood commercial areas and larger and auto-oriented commercial areas require different signage controls. By request, local communities may have local-option signage policies. The commercial area policy made some signs, including billboards, "non-conforming." Such nonconforming signs may continue to exist and may be repaired but may not be expanded.

Vail

As a meaningful element of public architecture, Vail has been undertaking a new signage program; the first phase, street and directional signage, has begun. This new effort has proved necessary despite the fact that the Town of Vail has had a sign ordinance since 1973, with several revisions and additions since then. Enforcement follows a usual pattern: Present application to the administrator, who reviews and then approves it. If a plan is disapproved, the applicant may alter the plan and resubmit the application or appeal to the design review board.

The sign administrator may approve signs up to 5 square feet in size or those made a part of a previously approved sign program. The design review board must receive monthly notification of all signs approved, and the board may review the administrator's decisions as well. Signs larger than 5 square feet must gain approval from the design review board. Vail's Town Council hears appeals of design review board refusals.

For the town of Vail, there are categories established which define the various types of signs and give specific requirements for each; the CC3 Zone District has its own regulations. Vail's sign ordinance has attempted to deal with signs that became nonconforming when the ordinance became effective, answering the query, "How do we get rid of them?" Termination of the right to display the signs occurs when they become obsolete (the advertised business is no longer viable), or if they are abandoned or destroyed. Signs that violate the ordinance must be immediately removed, and the town has the right to condemn a nonconforming sign. Any nonconforming sign that managed to avoid the above possibilities would have been phased out automatically five years after the ordinance came into being, that is, by 1982.

Conclusions

By examining how the 12 cities define the substantive element of signage, it is clear that they are basically concerned with two levels, (1) functional and (2) aesthetic, with more tendency toward aesthetics. Once again, the predominant criterion is "historical context and character" in most of the guidelines.

In some others, size and proportion and other microdesign elements become the major foci: The functional requirements may be essential from health, safety, and welfare points of view, but they are not extensively and adequately related to performance standards. Seldom do the guidelines and/or policies relate to the broader context of American culture and the proper role of signage from a guidance, commercial, or advertising aspect. Signs are an inevitable component of capitalism in America.

While tacky billboards scattered along a scenic road are not desirable, the use of signage as an integrated element in the urban texture can be very exciting. The city serves as a mode of communication; however, the American city does not function in the same way as the European city. "The American identity of place does not consist in a traditional system of urban spaces and permanent landmarks"; rather it relies on the expression of the architecture and its quality.[146] San Francisco counters this notion by seeking to eliminate those "characteristics which will cause new buildings to stand out in excess of their public importance." Perhaps we should stop apologizing for the things that do carry public importance in our society and begin to deal with signage as part of this culture rather than allow it to be just another element subject to rules of compatibility and fit.

This compatibility and fit are again the underlying premise if guidelines are heavily directed toward control of what is essentially considered undesirable, particularly in reference to billboards. Here, as in all the other categories of design, these notions pervade the literature. Irvine dismisses those things which are "non-harmonious with Irvine"; Kansas City attempts to improve "the visual continuity . . . through uniformity"; and Seattle judges a sign on the basis of "compatibility of the sign with character of the building." As with highways and parking, signage has not been considered an architectural element of the city. There is certainly a definite need for these guidelines to establish "order" in the city in addition to establishing the performance requirements. However, the critical issue is overemphasis on the correctional notion of what a sign is and what it could be by providing the opportunity for innovation and treatment of a necessary element as a work of art and as a part of the architecture of the city.

REFERENCE NOTES

1. Hamid Shirvani, *The Urban Design Process* (New York: Van Nostrand Reinhold, 1985).
2. Steven W. Hurtt, "The American Continental Grid: Form and Meaning," *Threshold* 2 (1983).
3. Christian Norberg-Schulz, *New World Architecture* (New York: Princeton Architectural Press, 1988), 30–31.

4. City of Seattle, "Mayor's Recommended Land Use and Transportation Plan for Downtown Seattle," May 1984, 36.
5. City of Portland, Bureau of Planning, "Recommended Central City Plan," January 1988, 16.
6. City of Minneapolis, City Planning Department and Downtown Council of Minneapolis, "Metro 2000 Plan," January 1988, 17.
7. City of Kansas City, City Development Department, "The Plaza Urban Design and Development Plan" (Discussion Draft), January 1988, 15.
8. Ibid., 45.
9. City of Kansas City, City Planning Division, "A City Plan for Urban Design and Development Policy" (Proposed), September 25, 1987.
10. City of Irvine, "City of Irvine General Plan," adopted August 1984 and updated August 1986.
11. Ibid., A-1.
12. City of Indianapolis, Department of Metropolitan Development, Division of Planning and Zoning, "Indianapolis 1980-2000: Regional Center Plan," UPP 770, August 1981.
13. Ibid., 40.
14. Vincent Ponte and Warren Travers, "Dallas Downtown Plan, 1986," City of Dallas and Central Dallas Association, 1986, Preface.
15. Ibid.
16. City of San Diego, Centre City Development Corporation, "Urban Design Program, Centre City San Diego," 1983, 27.
17. City of San Diego, "Southeast San Diego Planned District," Ordinance 0-16921 (new series), Section 103.1700, August 3, 1987, 1.
18. Ibid., Appendix A, 6.
19. Ibid., 10.
20. Hugh Ferriss, *The Metropolis of Tomorrow* (1929; reprint, Princeton, NJ: Princeton Architectural Press, 1986), 78-82.
21. Ibid., 82.
22. Gianni Vattimo, "Metropolis and Hermeneutics: An Interview," in *Beyond the City, the Metropolis*, ed. Georges Teyssot (Milan: Electa, 1988), 272.
23. Aldo Rossi, *Architecture and the City*, revised for the American Edition by Aldo Rossi and Peter Eisenman (Cambridge, MA: MIT Press, 1982), 60.
24. Pierluigi Nicolin, "Architecture Between Representation and Projects," in *Beyond the City, the Metropolis*, 273.
25. Elias Zenghelis, "The Aesthetics of the Present," *AD Profile* 72 (1988):66.
26. "Aspects and Limitations of Review and Submission Guidelines for Urban Design Review," approved by the [Lincoln] Urban Design Committee, July 1, 1981, and amended June 2, 1982, 2.
27. City of Portland, "Recommended Central City Plan," 22.
28. Ibid.
29. Ibid., 26.
30. Ibid.
31. Ibid., 64.
32. City of Kansas City, "The Plaza Urban Design and Development Plan," 86.

33. Ibid., 41.
34. Ibid., 82.
35. Ibid., 84.
36. City of Kansas City, *Zoning Ordinance,* Section 39.173, January 1987, 101.
37. Indianapolis-Marion County, "Indianapolis 1980-2000: Regional Center Plan," 28.
38. City of Baltimore, Department of Housing and Community Development, "Inner Harbor Project I Renewal Plan," originally approved June 15, 1967, and amended through May 8, 1985, 8, 15.
39. Ibid., 16.
40. City of Baltimore, Department of Housing and Community Development, "Urban Renewal Plan, Charles/North Revitalization Area," originally approved October 25, 1982, and amended through June 29, 1987, 7.
41. City of San Diego, "Urban Design Program, Centre City San Diego," 31-39.
42. Urban Land Institute, "Centre City San Diego," A Panel Advisory Service Report, January 18-23, 1987, 19.
43. Ibid.
44. Ibid., 22.
45. Ibid., 35.
46. City of San Francisco, City Planning Commission and Bernal Heights East Slope Preservation Committee, "Bernal Heights East Slope Building Guidelines," November 13, 1986, 12.
47. Ibid., 13.
48. Ibid., 16-18.
49. City of Seattle, Office of the Mayor, "Ballard Avenue Landmark District," February 1977, 4.
50. City of Seattle, City Council's Central Staff, "City of Seattle: Seattle 2000 Action Inventory," Final Working Draft, May 1985, V-37.
51. Ibid., V-41.
52. City of Minneapolis, "Metro 2000 Plan," 8.
53. Ibid., 11.
54. Ibid., 59.
55. Ibid., 59-60.
56. City of Minneapolis, Minneapolis Design Review Task Force, "Recommendations for a Design Review Process for the City of Minneapolis," December 10, 1983, 11-12.
57. City of Irvine, "City of Irvine General Plan," B5-6.
58. City of Dallas, Department of Urban Planning, "West End Historic District," 1977, 3.3.7.
59. City of Dallas, Bureau of Planning, "Near Eastside Conceptual Plan," May 1984 (from Ordinance 18312), 9-10.
60. John R. Stilgoe, *Common Landscape of America, 1580 to 1845* (New Haven, CT: Yale University Press, 1982), 129.
61. City of Baltimore, Baltimore City Planning Commission, "Baltimore's Development Program, 1988-1993," June 1987, 64.
62. Ibid., 65.
63. Ibid., 128.

64. Jean Gath, "West End Historic District, Dallas, Texas," a monograph in the Institute for Urban Design "Project Monograph Series," David Wallace, series editor, September 1986, Vol. 2, #2, 5.

65. City of Dallas, Department of Urban Planning, "Dallas Farmers Market Improvement Recommendations, Summary Report," August 1981, 1.

66. Ibid.

67. City of Dallas, Department of Planning and Development, "CBD Concept Plan," September 1983, 3.

68. Marion County, Indiana, "CBD Zoning Ordinance of Marion County, Indiana," originally passed in 1964 and amended in 1981, Chapter II, 2.01.A-17, 5.

69. City of Minneapolis, "Metro 2000 Plan," 9-11.

70. City of Kansas City, "The Plaza Urban Design and Development Plan," 63.

71. (Seattle) Municipal League Foundation, "Seattle Revisited," Findings of an Independent Citizen Review of the Seattle 2000 Goals, July 1, 1987, Vol. 1, 4-5.

72. Seattle City Council, "Land Use Policies for Neighborhood Areas," Resolution 27156, Sept. 4, 1984, 15.

73. Beatrice Ryan, "The Big Picture," *Planning* (February 1983):23-24.

74. Steve Dotterer, "Portland Arterial Street Classification Policy," in *Public Streets for Public Use,* ed. Anna Vernez Moudon (New York: Van Nostrand Reinhold, 1987), 170.

75. City of Portland, "Recommended Central City Plan," 18.

76. Ibid., 28.

77. Ibid., 36.

78. City of San Francisco, San Francisco Department of City Planning, "Downtown," proposal as adopted by the City Planning Commission as part of the "Master Plan," November 29, 1984, 97.

79. Dean L. Macris, "Memorandum to City Planning Commission," February 2, 1987, in "Rules for the 1986-87 Approval Period of the Office Development Limitation Program (Annual Limit)," as adopted by the City (of San Francisco) Planning Commission, Exhibit A, February 5, 1987, 8.

80. Ibid., 9.

81. Ibid., 10.

82. City of San Francisco, San Francisco Department of City Planning, "Downtown," 99.

83. Stilgoe, *Common Landscape,* 12.

84. Peter Eisenman, "The Futility of Objects," *Lotus International* 42, No. 2 (1984):67.

85. Franco Raggi, "City Without Design: A Fragmented Discourse," in *Beyond the City, The Metropolis,* 189.

86. Roger Scruton, "Public Space and the Classical Vernacular," in *The Public Face of Architecture,* ed. Nathan Glazer and Mark Lilla (New York: Free Press, 1987), 17.

87. City of Dallas, "CBD Concept Plan," 1.

88. City of Dallas, "Dallas Development Code," Ordinance 18968, Article X, "Landscape Regulations," 51-10.102, December 1985, 3.

89. Ibid., 4.

90. Ibid., 14.

91. City of Baltimore, "Baltimore Development Program, 1988–93," 58–59.

92. City of Baltimore, Baltimore Neighborhood Progress Administration, "Baltimore City Neighborhoods," 1987, 13.

93. Town of Vail, "Vail Village Design Considerations," June 11, 1980, iii.

94. Ibid., 3.

95. Ibid., 4.

96. City of San Diego, "Mid-City Community Plan," December 1984, 115.

97. Ibid., 117.

98. Ibid., 118.

99. City of San Diego, City Planning Department, "Centre City Urban Design Committee Final Report—Implementation," a memo to the Planning Commission concerning agenda of May 1, 1986, Item 4, April 28, 1986, 25.

100. City of Portland, Portland Bureau of Planning, "Recommended Central City Plan," 56.

101. Ibid., 124–125.

102. City of Seattle, "Seattle 2000 Action Inventory," V-34.

103. City of Seattle, "Summary of the Land Use and Transportation Plan for Downtown Seattle," November 1985, 22, 28.

104. City of Lincoln, Mayor's Ad Hoc Committee on Project Design, "Report," August 5, 1986, 5.

105. Frank Viviano and Sharon Silva, "Make No Little Plans," *TWA Ambassador* (January 1986):58.

106. Ibid., 59.

107. City of San Francisco, "Master Plan," "I. City-Wide Land Use Plan, A. Objectives," 1971, 1.1.

108. Ibid., B.1, 1.2.

109. Ibid., B.10.1.3.

110. Ibid., "Open Space," 10.9–.10.

111. City of Indianapolis, "Indianapolis 1980–2000: Regional Center Plan," v–vi.

112. Ibid., 16.

113. Ibid., 32.

114. Judy Hansen, memorandum to team members, "A City Plan [for Urban Design and Development Policy] (proposed), September 25, 1987, 14.

115. Ibid., 24.

116. Ibid.

117. Ibid., 25.

118. Ibid., 41.

119. Ibid., 44.

120. Ibid., 45.

121. City of Kansas City, "The Plaza Urban Design and Development Plan," 84–85.

122. City of Minneapolis, "Metro 2000 Plan," 8.

123. Ibid., 11.

124. City of Baltimore, "Inner Harbor Project I Renewal Plan," 11.

125. City of Baltimore, "Urban Renewal Plan Charles/North Revitalization Area," 12.

126. City of Indianapolis, Indianapolis Historic Preservation Commission, "Lockerbie Square Plan Development Standards," January 1987, D1.
127. Ibid., D48.
128. City of Irvine, "City of Irvine General Plan," A-13.
129. City of Irvine, "Sign Program Information Sheet," Form 42-01, PGJ 224-01/CDD (G), revised 10/2/67, 2.
130. City of Kansas City, "The Plaza Urban Design and Development Plan," 83.
131. Ibid., 88.
132. Ibid., 107.
133. "Lincoln-Lancaster County Comprehensive Plan," 1985, 222.
134. City of Minneapolis, "Zoning Code," Chapter 540.80, code 1960, as amended, 268.071, 3863.
135. Ibid., Chapter 540.90, Code 1960, as amended, 268.072, Ord. of 5-26-72, § 1, 3863–3864.
136. Ibid., Chapter 522.3000, Code 1960, as amended, § 251.280, 3726.
137. City of Portland, "Recommended Central City Plan," 80.
138. City of Portland, "Design Review Application & Submission Requirements," August 1984, 2.
139. City of San Diego, "Urban Design Program, Centre City San Diego."
140. City and County of San Francisco, "Downtown Plan," Ordinance 414-85, Section 1111.7, October 17, 1987, 93.
141. City of San Francisco, "Master Plan," 1971, 7.37.
142. Ibid., 7.43.
143. Ibid., 7.49.
144. City of Seattle, Ordinance 23.66.160.A, 3/5/85.
145. Ibid., C.
146. Norberg-Schulz, *New World Architecture,* 41.

Chapter **6**

Invention Versus Convention

As outlined in the beginning, the intention of this book is to illustrate the status of American public architecture at the present time through the study of its processes, organization, and essential premises; to critically evaluate the postmodern-based practice; and to identify the fundamental problems associated with the existing model. Doing so has rendered a picture of the current dichotomy between architecture of the city and architecture by the city.

In the Introduction, I outlined the general components of common practice into five groups; public evaluation, bureaucratic processes, framework and actors, context, and substantive elements. In Chapters 1 through 5 I have found, through critical assessment of each of these components comparing the 12 examined cities, that each city has a different yet not always distinct process of creating architecture in the public realm and many shared issues of concern. This chapter is an attempt to reiterate these issues of concern in each of the categories and relate them to a broader critical framework. The dichotomy that exists is clearly evident when this critical framework is applied to the reality of the 12 cities.

Many issues have been reviewed in each of the preceding chapters relating to specific components and elements of practice. However, several fundamental issues have been raised all across the range of categories of study. A careful reexamination of these common threads of inadequacy makes it clear that there are critical issues of postmodern practice of public architecture that must be addressed through the dialogue between policy and built form. The problems lie in certain shortcomings of history-based context, the inevitable generic design resulting from franchised service orientation, and the loss suffered in embracing convention versus invention.

6.1 HISTORY-BASED CONTEXT

Historic preservation is an obvious and extensive venue for the expansion of issues of contextualism through the methods of postmodern urban design methods. The thrust toward historic preservation is three-part: the commitment to preserving that which truly is part of the American social and cultural consciousness as it manifests itself through the built environment, the force of a district-focused agenda which aids in the cohesiveness and understanding of the structures in question as an urban context, and a reactionary stance to the loss of urban artifacts in the era of urban renewal.[1]

While preservation is an important part of the whole of public architecture, it is but one tactic in the development of urban fabric. The contextualist strategies of the 1970s sought to mediate between historicism and modernism (Figure 6.1). Tom Schumacher articulates this desire in saying, "To retreat to a hopelessly artificial past is unrealistic, but to allow a brutalizing system to dominate and destroy traditional urbanism is irresponsible."[2] Contextualism claimed to be just that middle ground. However, with the proliferation of guidelines and their prescriptive tendency, contextualism changes in meaning. Context becomes defined by the notion of history as context; the exploration of other layers of viable and significant context within the urban reality is discouraged in the attempt to rekindle the old city and its memories, however real or unreal they might be.

The language common to these guidelines, including those of our 12 cities, manifests this dependence upon design through compliance. Guide-

Figure 6.1. A prime example of history-based context in Minneapolis, where the new building is completely dominated by the building next to it.

lines are by nature static and are thus suited to the preservation of what already exists. The prescriptive format aids in the formula preservation of historic contexts. Often the definition of "historically significant" lies in the age of an object or building that becomes historic. Buildings of uncertain aesthetic, functional, and even historical quality then become a point of departure for subsequent development within the urban framework. A dubious relationship between age and significance, style and context has been fostered through the reliance on history as context.[3] While a feeling of loss in older neighborhoods and urban districts is surely justified, this type of preservation does little in regaining the reality of what is lost. Our brand of contextualism, although grounded in history, may be arbitrary or dysfunctional in terms of achieving an architecture of quality.[4] Historical allusion may be readily consumable by the general public, but it is not most relevant to the current urban fabric.

6.2 FRANCHISED SERVICE ORIENTATION

Guidelines tend to concentrate on new development within a given context of existing physical structure, using a limited brand of contextualism and the power of economic interests to guide the process. In becoming "givens" in the design guideline framework, there is the danger of stagnancy that obstructs urban dynamics and change. Master plans, comprehensive plans, and zoning ordinances are not quickly put into place within the bureaucratic machine; once implemented they may become (or are on the verge of being) outdated and not altered.[5] To compound the problem, many cities, as we have seen in our research here, often duplicate the procedures of another city. The static city is thus reestablished throughout the country. We must ask ourselves, given the universal nature of the guidelines, whether this process which we are on the verge of institutionalizing has anything to do with the historical reality of those cities we are trying to recapture. As Colin Rowe has illustrated, Rome is probably less a product of formal ordering than accommodation of fragments.[6]

6.3 CONVENTION VERSUS INVENTION

In approaching an urban architectural project by responding to the immediate or adjoining criteria implicit in conventional notions of context, the term urban design suggests the physical boundary of "the city," narrowly conceived. This is not, in short, the unlimited quality that encompasses the city and investigates the complete realm of data available to the site. Public architecture which can acknowledge this quality through individual (and perhaps individualistic) buildings is preferable.[7] Conveying the typical postmodern stance, Robert Stern defines architecture as "less an issue of innovation than an act of interpretation; to be an architect is to possess an individual voice speaking a generally understood language."[8] Design elements provide a vocabulary, not a framework; as we have attempted in this book, we must reexamine our vision of the city in history—in its cultural context.

The illustration and reiteration of the above critical issues of postmodern models of practice presents us with the fact that never in the history of architecture and planning in this country has there been such an overemphasis and acceptance of conventional models (Figure 6.2). Contemporary public architecture is marked by a conservative attitude toward the accepted norm, conventions that are based on passé, outdated notions of what a city should or could be. Unmistakedly, this is the only period when architectural disciplines are at the complete service of established power, the market. The irony is, however, that the market does not necessarily define this service orientation; on the contrary, the market is searching for invention and innovative ideas. The problem, then, is that there have been few innovative ideas and concepts for perhaps the last three decades. The profession has had to endure a struggle between popular planning as an institution and the power of economic

Figure 6.2. A prime example of a postmodern covered shopping mall in downtown Baltimore which has been copied in numerous other cities.

interests. Only recently has architecture moved toward a critical consideration of the use of convention in solving the problem of public architecture, but the prevailing attitude of postmodern conservatism has been flourishing and expanding as rapidly as ever before.

It is therefore critical to focus on rethinking and reevaluating our disciplines. We must move to an innovative, forward-looking mode. In the final chapter of this book, I will be outlining some ingredients of future public architecture.

REFERENCE NOTES

1. Hamid Shirvani, "Architecture and the City: The Divergence," in *Who Designs America?* A selection of papers presented at the 76th Annual Meeting of the Association of Collegiate Schools of Architecture 1988 (Washington D.C.: Association of Collegiate Schools of Architecture, 1988), 135-41; idem, "Architecture Versus Franchised Design," *Urban Design and Preservation Quarterly* 11, No. 2/3 (1988):2-8.
2. Tom Schumacher, "Contextualism: Urban Ideals + Deformations," *Casabella* 359-360 (1971):81.
3. See Note 1.
4. Shirvani, "Architecture and the City: The Divergence," 140.
5. Ibid.
6. Colin Rowe, *Collage City* (Cambridge, MA: MIT Press, 1978).
7. Shirvani, "Architecture and the City: The Divergence," 135-41.
8. Robert A. M. Stern, "Introduction: Modern Traditionalism," in *Robert A. M. Stern: Buildings and Projects, 1981-1985,* ed. Luis F. Rueda (New York: Rizzoli, 1986), 6.

Chapter 7

ARCHITECTURE OF THE CITY

The city as an advertising and self-advertising structure, as an ensemble of channels of communication, becomes a sort of machine emitting incessant messages: indeterminacy itself is given specific form and offered as the only determinateness possible for the city as a whole. In this way form is given to the attempt to make the language of development live, to make it a concrete experience of everyday life.[1]

The above statement by Tafuri is perhaps the best definition of a context for the architecture *of* or *in* the American city. This context somehow elaborates Max Weber's theory explaining the form of the American city.[2] The question we have been avoiding (or perhaps we have not responded to it clearly) is how to deal with what I call "free form of the city," the city of constant transformation, the American city. I purposely refuse to call this chaos, although some of my colleagues have been inspired by the work of James Gleick[3] and have expanded prolifically upon this notion. My refusal is often semantic and not rational. I feel chaos has a connotation of something unpleasant, a confusion stemming from an inherent evil.

However, order is associated with good because it is easily recognized and comprehended with an understanding based on "a quick apprehension through the eye, an ocular taking, a possession by sight."[4] While readily intelligible, order is considered the pursuit of intellectuals.

I do not feel that the American city and its metropolitan areas are chaotic, nor do I agree with Colin Rowe that there is an order to be found in chaos where it exists. I feel the American cities are moving cities; they are, as Tafuri points out, cities with an indeterminacy that need not be defined by a hidden order. Understanding and responding to such fluidity is the real challenge of our intelligence and lies ahead of us, for it represents that which is not easily assimilated into our present knowledge. Obviously, the structuralist manifesto of modern architecture has failed to deal with this mobility.

The process-oriented, socially superficial, touchy-feely facades and arcades created in accordance with the history-based context of postmodernism are proving to be both inappropriate and uninspiring. This book has been an attempt to demonstrate this failure in a detailed way, furthering many lines of questioning beyond the general conceptual ideologies involved to the operational levels of day-to-day activities. We have identified many problems with the current state of public architecture. The critical question, which is beyond the scope of this book, is where to go from here. As a closing thought, however, I would like to offer a proposal for a direction, a conceptual and general outline rather than a specific and detailed solution. Clearly, based on the above arguments, any specific and detailed proposal would be inappropriate and superficial.

This proposal is therefore simply a series of *notes* which require a composer to arrange them into a well-orchestrated piece. The composer in this case is the architect, broadly conceived. My proposal is uncomplicated yet poses difficult issues that need to be addressed. It includes six points which I believe are crucial aspects of the *notes* that constitute the architecture of the city: nature, context, process, craft, invention, and institution. The simplicity of my proposal stems from its conceptual nature. Complexity lies in the fact that the architect as composer has to be able to create a piece of exquisite music, to build a crafted piece within and as part of this culture of fragments. The process involves the exploration of existing context including time, place, people, market, and all the other ingredients that add to this ever-changing composition. We move beyond the comfort of the classical notions of order and beauty to the real and often confusing nature of the world, both beautiful and ugly. This is based on my definition of the American city as a "landscape of fragments."

The art involved in this process of public architecture resides in the ability to add to this landscape and explore new inventions while attempting to mediate between the existing and additional fragments, in addition to dealing with functional requirements of space and time. This mediation goes beyond the narrow definition of traditional context. It means the American city must deal with the automobile rather than hide or ban it; must deal with pop culture and the commercial strip rather than deny its cultural significance or camouflage it with postmodern quotation; must accept and deal with suburbanization and scattered development rather than covering it with the application of European notions of urbanism; and must deal with mobility of capital and labor and other characteristics of a democratic and capitalist society. It must come to terms with what Tafuri sees as the struggle of public architecture within the capitalist framework: the concurrent circumstances of the mode of building production diminishing the role of architectural ideology and the contradiction between social and economic concerns which might halt the capitalist progression.[5] Having said all this, let me discuss what I mean by each of the ingredients I have referred to above.

7.1 NATURE

... nature and architecture, nature and the artificial are now inseparably bound together, are now part of the same tangle, of the same landscape ... it is no longer possible to separate them but reproposing an ideological and metaphysical distinction, which, however, does not take into consideration what is, by now, our experience of the world ... we no longer have any view of any landscape, not even of a flower in the mountains or of a cloud, which is not determined, in some way or other, by our experience of the artificial. ...[6]

Nature in the American context has several meanings. Its landscape is certainly one of the most beautiful settings in the world, one that provides almost every possible natural condition from flat plains to mountains, desert to seaside, frigid temperatures to extreme heat. A variety of climates and terrains means an abundance of natural resources for a variety of uses.

Nature plays an important part in the determination of the landscape of fragments. In fact, it is because of the availability of resources in this magnificent landscape that development of individual and group dwellings, villages, towns, and cities of different sizes and function is also possible. Again it is nature and the vast landscape that provides the possibility of individual land ownership and spirit of a free country. Therefore, while the development of cities and regions has had adverse impacts on the natural landscape, the landscape itself has been the major determinant for such development. There is no doubt that there are limited resources; therefore, the development of cities and suburbs must be sensitive to nature and resources. Our natural environment, however, sits precariously at the center of a struggle, fluctuating at the hand of humans between remaining a sanctuary untouched, or at least unharmed, and a resource for the taking.

The environmental movements of the 1960s and the work of Ian McHarg and his followers have certainly had a great deal of impact in incorporating natural and ecological issues into the process of design and development. However, as we have demonstrated in this book, this set of issues has been treated superficially by many cities. Environmental impact studies are good technical reports, but they are dry; they do respond to the "soul" of the project. They do not give the architect the feeling and understanding of the ecology of the city and region.

My proposal for "nature" as a note of composition seeks to move beyond this struggle for supremacy between human and nature or the artificial reconciliation that current methods offer. Given the present condition of our landscape with nature and the artificial "inseparably bound together," we must move away from the dialectical relationship of human/nature, technology/nature. We must require the architect and the city to feel, smell, taste, and see the ecology of the place; the nature and ecology of the landscape; the stuff of which the landscape of fragments, both artificial and natural, consists; the industrial landscape and the people. Design guidelines cannot provide such information. While they lend themselves to the documentation and verification of physical data of the city and its resources, they do not help interpret the other layers of nature in a city. The environmental impact report, if not treated superficially or put together lightly, can provide a basis of information; it can set the limits, yet it cannot provide a feel for the landscape.

Nature also has played a role in the ideological framework of architecture through an interplay of the concept of nature and the art and craft of architecture. Though, in the history of architecture, nature has played a significant role in the creation of architecture and urban form, there is a lack of such inspirational notes in today's music of architecture. Many of the investigatory proposals of the nineteenth and twentieth centuries suggest that architecture and nature are in fact interconvertible. This paradigm can be traced through history all the way to Leon Krier's formula for "2 Kinds of Roofs" (1974). This rediscovery of nature through architecture is based on a vision of a world archetype of mathematical and architectonic nature, or architectural monuments to nature.[7]

Such an archetypal relationship, however, does not exist in the contemporary landscape where the artificial and the natural overlap and comingle in both the physical realm and the spiritual interpretation of their reality. The rediscovery of nature in architecture today cannot be achieved through monuments to nature or through crediting it as the natural origin of architectural elements.

7.2 CONTEXT

The fragmentation of our contemporary, "mad" condition inevitably suggests new and unforeseen regroupings of its fragments. No longer linked in a coherent whole, independent from their past, these autonomous fragments can be recombined through a series of permutations whose rules have nothing to do with those of classicism or modernism.[7]

My proposal for the use of context as a note in the architectural composition is a consideration of context as rule versus context as text. In perceiving context as rule, a collection of clandestine operations that determine the connection between a given architectural proposal and its environs, there is the risk of limiting the contextual investigations to the purely physical realm. Context as rule in public architecture is implemented by various central mechanisms such as zoning ordinances, land-use regulations, and density and occupancy mix standards. Perceiving context as the word implies, a text or syntactical discourse, gives it freedom void of the prescriptive quality of rules. Foucault reminds us that ". . . any limit we set may perhaps be no more than an arbitrary division made in a constantly mobile whole."[9]

Considered as text, context then becomes an object void of preassigned meaning; it is able then to participate in the abstractions that are available to the other elements of architecture. In this way the architect becomes what Derrida calls the "architect-weaver": "He plots grids, twining the threads of a chain, his writing holds out a net. A weave always weaves in several directions, several meanings, and beyond meaning."[10]

At present there is a dichotomy between the semantical and syntactical approach within the text of public architecture.

> The semantical approach deals with the buildings as an independent element with its own context and meaning determining structure and form, while the syntactical method deals with the building as a mutating undefinable entity within a shifting urban context.[11]

Libeskind challenges the emphasis on semantics by reminding us that

> the presumption that space can be treated as a system of coordinates, an empty cage . . . is a tautology without depth or horizon. It is a reflection of a false identity in which space itself really means nothing and yet is predestined for our own use.[12]

However, in contemporary design practice this "cage" has been misinterpreted as the contextual basis for design.[13]

7.3 PROCESS

Process is a generic term. According to Webster's *Third New International Dictionary*, process is

> the action of moving forward progressively from one point to another on the way to completion. . . . The action of continuously going along through each of a succession of acts, events, or developmental stages. . . .[14]

In architecture, urban design, and planning disciplines, the term *process* has established a notion of "participatory decision-making," which is a rather narrow definition of the term. Process-oriented design is a term that emerged in the 1960s and has been used extensively thereafter, particularly in planning and urban design as well as architecture. The term itself and the ideas that form its basic framework have also permeated architectural education in the United States. In its extreme sense, process orientation attempts to form a framework which through the participation of actors and users generates a design proposal based on consensus, or what I call the town meeting/democracy approach to design. The designer, be he or she architect, urban designer, or other professional, may inevitably become a "mechanical artist" rather than an inventor of a new craft or architecture. A criticism of this notion has been made adequately in this book. Here, I would like to propose a different notion, exemplifying the real meaning of the word *process* and its application to the architecture of the city.

In my view, the process in the architecture of the city is part of the whole of urban and regional planning change, part of its transformation and thus the societal process of which architecture is a part. Architecture has to explore this societal process, understand it, and respond to it rather than simply answer to the client, at the service of the power, the capital. Architecture should inform and educate the public by sharing the exploration of this process of social change and its transformation into the craft of architecture. A process of material production, a generation of physical form responsive to a time or period of this societal change is, I believe, an essential ingredient of the architecture of the city.

Considering this notion in a broader sense, the process of formation and production of architecture should be part of the broader system of social process and thus cannot simply travel into the twilight zone, attempting to produce an outdated history-based form that needs no explanation to the public.

My notion of process is sequential decisions and action that can cope with the mobile nature of the United States. The process has to spontaneously deal with the ever-changing condition of city development. It perhaps should be a step ahead and a part of the change. By this I am not referring to goal-oriented master plans that by the time they are realized are already outdated. Such ideas are based on process-oriented design. My notion is process-integrated design with process referring to broader socio-cultural changes.

7.4 CRAFT

Craft is perhaps the most important aspect of architecture of the city. It is the "soul" of the discipline and separates architecture from the other service disciplines. Unfortunately the element of craft has been weakened tremendously in the post-1960s era. Mass production of urban elements, that which the introduction of craft in the later early modern movements tried to discourage, has replaced craft. It has been said by many that "architecture is the mother art." Accepting this singular definition of architecture, craft then is the soul of this mother art. According to Walter Behrendt, "only architecture can give clear ideological guidance to the crafts. . . . Architects create relationships in space, which is what produces an integrated theme in their work."[15]

In the history of architecture, the return to a craftsman orientation was for the most part a reactionary stance in response to the isolation of the worker from his or her product brought about by the Industrial Revolution and the social conditions that accompanied it. The early craft movements, while not wholly successful in their attempts to create handcrafted objects of integrity for the middle class due to the high cost of construction, did give pause to the sweeping changes resulting from the mass production of goods. The value of craft was instilled in these early modernist movements, and an attempt was made about the turn of the century to reconcile the human with the machine. With the development of industry and the twentieth century social change, the Germans were the first group to have made a significant effort to blend craft with the realities of the industrial age, creating a new notion of craftsmanship within the context of industry. The Bauhaus school was the outgrowth of the Deutsche Werkbund, promoting this notion in architecture, industrial arts, and city planning.

This approach was exported to the United States during World War II and has influenced the design of objects, architecture, and urban complexes. However, the ties to the often self-conscious expressions of the Modern movement and its rejection brought about the move toward process-oriented design and destroyed the notion of craft by association. The assemblage of historical quotations in a plastic collage and the current market-responsive commercial craft can hardly be deemed sufficient alternatives. In the post-modern era, industry has usurped craft and turned it into codified, packaged, franchised design, as witnessed in the discussions in this book. As a result the mother art is left without the very soul which elevates her above the other arts. The essential necessity of the architecture of the city is the notion of craft in city objects, buildings, and fragments. Without craft, architecture is nothing more than a mechanical art, attempting to deal with function and market with an afterthought facade. Without craft we have been rebuilding cities without soul. The plasticity of covered malls and manicured trees does not provide the true work of art, the soul.

7.5 INVENTION

Impatience . . . might come to those who, drenched in Classical desire, would wish that architecture were easy. Frustration will come to those who think that the rules of architecture and its procedures can and should be codified, and that the practice of architecture therefore can be transmitted through the following of known rules. Irritation may come to those who believe that the significance of architecture can be known antecedently. And angry will be those who tire of grand questions and deny them.[16]

John Whiteman thus describes the discomfort that accompanies the breaking of convention in architectural exploration. Convention is that which is easily assimilated into our current understanding. Invention is that which is not and therefore requires a sensitivity of understanding and a need for contemplation.

Invention is not simply novelty, but it is not, on the other hand, the disassociation of originality and creativity. Brent Brolin suggests that creativity should "stress refinement within the aesthetic confines of the given visual context, whether that is modern or traditional."[17] Others suggest that conventionality is a public right, using this to justify the construction of buildings that will not intimidate their surroundings. When, however, do these aesthetic and cultural values of the surrounding buildings threaten the dynamic of the city? If we simply move ahead in building technology but refuse to allow the invention of the form and substance of architecture itself, with what will we be left?

7.6 PUBLIC INSTITUTION

The city is a public institution, and therefore its architecture should be responsive to the public. This cannot be achieved through education of both the architect and the public. It should be a part of the architect's ethical code, just like any other discipline; an architect cannot simply serve the market and the client. As a social discourse, his or her overall responsibility is to serve the public. However, we do not serve the public merely by not dong them a disservice. Architecture must not only respond; it must also lead in its service and aesthetic capacity.

If we are to reform the present practice of public architecture, we have to call for educational reform in our architectural and planning curriculums. We also have to educate the public in regard to art and architecture. It is only through raising the level of consciousness of art, craft, and architecture that we can achieve an American city based on American values but achieved through the process of invention and craft responsive to societal change.

REFERENCE NOTES

1. Manfredo Tafuri, *Architecture and Utopia, Design and Capitalist Development* (Cambridge, MA: MIT Press, 1976), 166-169.
2. Max Weber, *The City* (New York: Free Press, 1958), 11-19.

3. James Gleick, *Chaos* (New York: Viking, 1988).

4. John Whiteman, "On Classical Representation of the Human Soul and Its Denial," in *Investigations in Architecture*, ed. Jonathan Jova Marvel (Cambridge, MA: Harvard Graduate School of Design, 1986), 6.

5. Tafuri, 170.

6. Alessandro Massarente, "Architecture and Nature, Interview with Franco Rella," *Utopia* 2 (1988):22.

7. Werner Oechslin, "Architecture and Nature, On the Origin and Convertibility of Architecture," *Lotus* 31 (1981):11.

8. Bernard Tschumi, *Cinegram Folie Le Park De La Villette* (Princeton, NJ: Architecture Press), 24.

9. Michel Foucault, *The Order of Things* (New York: Vintage Books, 1970), 50.

10. Jacques Derrida, "Point de Folie—Maintenant L'Architecture," Bernard Tschumi, "La Case Vide—La Villette, 1985," *AA Files* 12 (Summer 1986):73.

11. Hamid Shirvani, "Context as Coherence in Discourse," *Urban Design and Preservation Quarterly* 12, No. 1/2 (1989):38.

12. Daniel Libeskind, *Between Zero and Infinity* (New York: Rizzoli, 1981), 28.

13. Hamid Shirvani, "Context as Coherence in Discourse," 32-38.

14. *Webster's Third New International Dictionary*, s.v. "process."

15. Walter Behrendt, "The State of Arts and Crafts," in *Die Form* I (1925-6):37-40.

16. John Whiteman, "On Classical Representation of the Human Soul and Its Denial," 11.

17. Brent Brolin, "Architecture in Context: Fitting New Buildings with Old," *The Harvard Architecture Review* 2 (1981):20.

Index

663-1600

FEB/8